THROUGH THE YEAR WITH MICHAEL RAMSEY

THROUGH THE YEAR WITH MICHAEL RAMSEY

Devotional readings for every day

edited by
MARGARET DUGGAN

WILLIAM B. EERDMANS PUBLISHING COMPANY

Library of Congress Cataloging in Publication Data

Ramsey, Arthur Michael, Abp. of Canterbury,
    1904-
    Through the year with Michael Ramsey.
    1.   Devotional calendars — Church of England.
I.   Duggan, Margaret.   II.   Title.
BV4811.R28   1976   242'.2   76-49556
ISBN 0-8028-3494-9

CONTENTS

ACKNOWLEDGMENTS

I should like to express my gratitude to Longmans, Green & Co., Ltd, SCM, and SPCK for permission to quote copyright material. I have loved doing this book, not least because of the helpfulness and generosity I have had from Dr. Ramsey. But I am also grateful to Lady Ramsey for her hospitality and interest; to my husband for his patient readiness to help; and to my friend, Peter Wyld, who, after seven years of editorial work together, still cannot resist subbing my copy and reading my proofs.

Key to acknowledgments in the text

CP   — *Canterbury Pilgrim*, SPCK
SS   — *Sacred and Secular*, Longmans
CEA — *Canterbury Essays and Addresses*, SPCK
DEA — *Durham Essays and Addresses*, SPCK
CPT — *The Christian Priest Today*, SPCK
GCW — *God, Christ and the World*, SCM
ICF   — *Introducing the Christian Faith*, SCM
MP   — *Meaning of Prayer*, SPCK
BR   — *Beyond Religion* SPCK
ION — *Image Old and New*, SPCK
FFF — *Freedom, Faith and the Future*, SPCK

INTRODUCTION

If I was asked to define Anglican spirituality I would immediately think of Michael Ramsey. He is fully in the mainstream of the great Anglican divines. He is also truly radical. Everything he says or writes he has thought out from its very roots. Every belief he holds has been tested by his intellect, and intellectually he is a giant among men.

The most obvious thing about him is the strength of his belief in God and his love of Jesus Christ, and the vividness of his priesthood. And yet through it—Anglican-style—there runs a sufficient streak of scepticism to make him very sensitive to the difficulties of the unbeliever. Modestly, hesitantly, and with deep sympathy, he will say that he thinks he "knows what it is like" not to be able to believe in God. And it is this quality, a faith which is so much a part of him, and yet always "an adventure of ceaseless battling . . . a costly peace and serenity in the midst of conflict" which makes him so attractive to Christians and non-Christians, Anglicans and others, who are searching among their doubts for glimpses of the eternal truth.

Michael Ramsey's Christianity is not cosy or "safe", but it is hugely generous, strong, and full of assurances about the goodness of God. Heaven is very real to him as the ultimate fulfilment of our present existence; and he looks forward to it as the greatest adventure of all. Yet he doesn't claim to know what it is like. Always his intellectual honesty is wrestling with traditional faith, and always he is growing.

In compiling this anthology, and in getting to know him better, I have been fascinated by this continual growth. It is part of his radicalism. He preaches a very coherent gospel: indeed, I have found almost identical passages time and again among his addresses and writings; and yet no new idea has ever passed him by without being seriously explored to see whether it contains some new insight or element of truth to be added to his own understanding and teaching.

Nor has he been afraid to admit to changing his mind or expanding his ideas. He is now very ready to say that he reacted both too quickly and too harshly to the publication of *Honest to God*, and had also very quickly, to modify his first criticism of it. Conversely, however, not even the most strident public criticism could make him budge when standing on a matter of principle. A tornado beat about his ears in 1965 when he said in the House of Lords that he thought the use of British troops would be justified to quell the UDI rebellion in Rhodesia and to protect African interests. He felt all the savagery of the reaction, but a fortnight later he was heard to say that he would be prepared to make the same statement again.

And yet, through it all, Arthur Michael Ramsey, hundredth Archbishop of Canterbury, Primate of all England, acknowledged leader of the world-wide Anglican Communion of Churches, has remained the shyest and most sensitive of men. His stammering image on television has often obscured, for those who do not know him, the warmth, the intellect, and the wit which has so endeared him to those who know him better in contexts where he is confident and relaxed. But even for those who have frequent occasion to meet him, the lack of small talk, the shy man's inhibition (so easily misunderstood) about showing interest in the personal lives of his acquaintances, his uncanny habit of "switching off" and simply not hearing any irrelevancy introduced into the conversation, can be disconcerting.

Since early middle age he has looked venerable—not always to the benefit of his public image. But in recent years the eccentric eyebrows which almost, but not quite, hide the twinkle, the strong features, the white-fringed tonsure, and the good-humoured reactions which can so easily explode into laughter against himself, have been a photographer's and cartoonist's delight.

But the shyness, the stammer, the vulnerable sensitivity, remain basically unchanged even by thirteen years in one of the most exposed and isolated jobs in the world. To be Archbishop of Canterbury is to be seen by the common man as the ultimate spokesman and representative of that most amorphous of bodies, the Church of England. He is expected, by the great conservative masses which make up most of the population of England, to hold all the "traditional" conservative views inherited from the puritanical moralism of the last century and to equate morals with sexual behaviour and conventional law and order. And he is *not* expected to give—as Michael Ramsey has given—as much or even more attention to those other moral issues of political violence, racialism, and social justice.

Yet the Archbishop of Canterbury is not protected by a Curia, and his words technically carry only the authority of his own Christian wisdom and experience. He is frequently attacked, abused, and ridiculed. He can be caught off his guard in an impromptu interview by the press or on television, for the media expect him always to be available, and make demands on him that they make on no other church leader. And however great his personal humility—and Ramsey's is very great indeed—there is a section of the public who always insist that he must be a self-styled model of Christian perfection, and thereupon take a malicious relish in spotting the human flaws, or seeing any deviation from convention as a fall from grace.

How has Michael Ramsey, now living a retired life as a priest and scholar near his old theological college of Cuddesdon, survived all this while continuing to grow in understanding both of the things of this world and of the things of God? What made him the man that he is? He says that he does not want a biography written in his lifetime, but there is plenty of fascinating material for a sensitive biographer.

He was a solitary and, he says, rather eccentric little boy. He was born in 1904, the son of a Cambridge don and mathematician. It was a pious household; his father was a Congregationalist, son of a Congregational minister, and his mother was an Anglican, the daughter of a parson. There were family prayers and strong Christian teaching, but the children were free to choose their denominational allegiance.

For a while the young Michael had a penchant for the pious children's books of the time, sentimental stories about the poor with titles like *Jessica's First Prayer*. Then he discovered the delights of Henty and began his lifelong interest in history. He was, he says, "the rather dull boy" growing up in the shadow of his brilliant brother, Frank, two years older, who was to become a mathematician and philosopher, and to die at the age of twenty-seven.

In the early days Michael attended his father's church, but at school at Repton (where his predecessor as Archbishop of Canterbury, Geoffrey Fisher, was then headmaster) he finally opted for the Anglican Church and was confirmed in it, though he didn't escape the usual period of late-adolescent doubts.

At Cambridge, reading classics, his political ambitions flared. In 1926 he was President of the Cambridge Union, and saw himself being called to the bar before making a career in Liberal politics. But halfway through his university time, influenced in some degree by William Temple who was conducting a mission at the university, he recognised a superficiality in his political interests, and turned to theology as something profound enough to satisfy his deepest needs. He got a First Class theological degree, and then went to Cuddesdon College to prepare for the priesthood.

Two weeks after he arrived at Cuddesdon his mother was killed in a car accident. He knew all the desolation of loss, for her influence had been great, and it was her Anglicanism he had chosen as his way of life. The grief immensely deepened the experience of the sensitive young ordinand, and whatever understanding and compassion the later Professor, Bishop, or Archbishop has shown towards human suffering started growing from that time. "Christians can't offer an intellectual explanation of suffering," he says, "but they do have something to say about it derived from Christ crucified."

His mother's death was followed all too soon by that of his brother who died of a liver disease. Frank was not a believing Christian, though he did have some feeling for mysticism; and it was with him that Michael learned so much of the respect and understanding that he had always shown towards the honest unbeliever.

He was ordained and served two curacies, in Liverpool and in Boston, Lincolnshire. He remembers the experiences as enjoyable, but probably of more value to him than to the parishioners. His reputation as a curate has lingered in one of them where his confirmation classes were much admired, but the effect was spoiled by his inability to recognise members of his class when he met them in the street. (In latter years, however, his memory for faces once seen has become phenomenal.) And it was during this time that he also had his only experience of schoolmastering: in both Liverpool and Lincoln he taught in the local primary school. "I expect it was a bit of a joke," he says now.

After two years of parish work he was back in the academic world; and by 1940, when he was thirty-six years old, he was Canon of Durham Cathedral and Professor of Divinity at the University. He loved his time in Durham, then, and later when he became Bishop there. He felt a great sense of identification with the Christianity of the north, with Bede and Cuthbert, and the rugged Durham miners. But at this time he was first and foremost and all the time an academic theologian. He always saw theology and scholarship as part of the priesthood, and his early political enthusiasms, and Temple's influence, made him keep an eye on the social application of the Gospel. But the real awareness of the world's issues, the perfectly integrated concern for this world and the next together, was not to flower—and then so abundantly—until he got to Canterbury.

11

It was while he was Canon of Durham that he married Joan Hamilton, a lively radical in her own right, and secretary to the suffragan bishop who lived two doors away. They moved briefly to Cambridge where he was Regius Professor, and then in 1952 came the invitation to be Bishop of Durham. It was the hardest decision he ever had to make—to leave university life to become a diocesan bishop. It took him a fortnight to make up his mind, and if it had been any but the beloved see of Durham being offered, he might well have refused. His later translations from Durham to York, and from York to Canterbury, he accepted quickly. "Once I had made the decision to become a bishop, I went where I was pushed."

He also enjoyed the northerness of York, an archbishopric very different from that of Canterbury, without anything of the same exposure. And still his writings and addresses were very much that of an academic and a teacher: a profound and memorable teacher, (for I have come across people with treasured memories of his retreat addresses when he was still a popularly unknown Canon of Durham), but the huge latching on to the concerns of the world had still to come.

He followed Archbishop Fisher to Canterbury in 1961. ("Suddenly you find you are Archbishop of Canterbury, and no one is more surprised and amused than yourself.") He was still comparatively little known by the Church in the south, and he had to plunge right in to one of the most turbulent decades of our social history. Almost immediately public controversy raged round the new theology, the "new morality", permissiveness, violence, and the racial tensions. An archbishop constantly on the demanding end of the mass media had to keep his head, and Michael Ramsey kept his by the openness of his mind, the clearness of his intellect, and the sureness of his spiritual faith.

Immediately, too, he became the most peripatetic of archbishops, and to read the list of the countries he visited make his archiepiscopate sound like a continual circumnavigation not only of the Anglican Communion, but of the world-wide Christian Church. He was a president of the World Council of Churches in Delhi and in Sweden. He lectured in America many times. He visited a score of countries as diverse as Bulgaria, South America, East Germany, and Fiji. He was—a great moment in history—the official guest of the Pope in 1966. ("Yes, I liked him very much as a man, very much. His mind was young and lively then.") And in 1970 he was in South Africa having a private and "grim" interview with Prime Minister Vorster on the subject of *apartheid*.

At home his strongly expressed views on the need to build up good relationships with the coloured communities in Britain led Harold Wilson to ask him to be chairman of the National Committee for Commonwealth Immigrants, and as such he spoke vigorously in the House of Lords on behalf of the Kenya Asians. He was also very outspoken about Rhodesia, about the bombing in Vietnam, about abortion, divorce, and capital punishment, and in favour of the Wolfenden proposals on homosexuality. And there is no reason why such speeches should come to an end yet for, with a life peerage, he can continue to play a full part in Lords' debates.

He was constantly busy ecumenically. When he came to Canterbury he had hoped to make relationships with the Eastern Orthodox Churches his special ecumenical interest, for he had an almost lifelong sympathy with Orthodox spirituality. But though he indeed strengthened personal relationships with their leaders, everything about the Eastern Churches moves so slowly that it would now not surprise him if an Anglican *rapprochement* with Rome came first. In England he has been an affectionately regarded and acknowledged leader among all the Churches, and his greatest disappointment was the final failure of the Anglican-Methodist Reunion Scheme on May 3, 1972. On that sadly memorable day, when the General Synod met specially to accept or reject the scheme, Archbishop Ramsey was at his most magnificent. The passionate sincerity of his address to Synod was powerful enough to convert a few of the diehard opponents to the scheme. But not quite enough. Synod was committed to union only if there was an overall majority of 75 per cent, but the figure attained was 68·81.

I have found it wonderful that while he was involved in all this, getting more and more caught up in the complications of national and world issues, his sermons and religious writings became ever simpler, more profound, more direct: love God and love man; sacrifice and glory go together; heaven is the meaning of it all. It is also an interesting facet of this "simplicity in profundity" that his theological books have been very slight in size. The writing of weighty volumes have never been his métier, which makes him unusual among theologians, and perhaps proves what a very good religious teacher he is—especially when it comes to students. He has continued to give as much time as he could to talking with students —to his and their mutual enjoyment—and many of the passages in this anthology have been drawn from those occasions.

I hope that in my selection from his writings and addresses you may find as I have the essential goodness of this great Christian's teaching. For me, in these past months, I have felt I have been handling pure gold, and my dearest hope is that a little of it rubbed off on my fingers and will stay with me permanently.

Margaret Duggan
Winchester
May 1975

JANUARY

THE UNENDING ADVENTURE   January 1

People sometimes ask me if I have ever felt like losing my faith. No: my faith is always part of me. But faith isn't a state of easy and calm security. It is an adventure of ceaseless battling with troubles: a peace of mind and a serenity indeed, but a costly peace and serenity in the midst of conflict.

After all, our world is a world of conflict, and faith is not an escape from it, but something which—in St. John's words—"overcomes it".

LIFE MAY BE TURNED INSIDE OUT   January 2

The presence of Jesus brings joy and peace to those who experience it. But it never brings comfort without also bringing a gift so generous that we cannot bear it as it is so shattering to our pride, and without also bringing a costly demand upon our minds and actions.

Jesus being with us where we are means our being with him where he is. If Jesus is with you, what is he demanding of you— urgently—in your actions about poverty, or peace, or race, or your

15

neighbour? If Jesus is with you, he will not let you wear blinkers about your relations with your fellows. If Jesus is with you, your life may be turned inside out.

GLORY AND SACRIFICE GO TOGETHER   January 3

The sovereignty of Jesus is the sovereignty of love, self-sacrifice, self-giving. The Cross and the Ascension go together.

We remember how in the Gospel of St. John the phrase *lifting-up* refers both to Calvary and the Ascension, linking the two together. We remember how the word *glory* refers both to Calvary and to heaven. We remember how in the Apocalypse the *lamb* and the *throne* go together.

What a symbol is there! The lamb stands for sacrifice—the self-sacrifice of Jesus—the throne stands for sovereignty. The power in the world by which evil is overcome is the self-sacrifice of Jesus. The only divine omnipotence is the omnipotence of sacrificial love.

NOT SERVANTS BUT FRIENDS   January 4

Christianity has at its centre the intense personal allegiance of Christ's followers to him. While it includes a doctrine and implies a philosophy, it is in essence a Person.

Nowhere is this more vividly presented than in the discourse at the Last Supper in the Gospel of St. John, where the intensity of the relationship between the disciples and their Lord is seen in such imagery as "I am the vine, you are the branches; abide in me and I in you", and "I have not called you servants, but friends".

BEYOND THE LIMITS OF SPACE OR TIME   January 5

In his ministry on earth, those who would be with Jesus must needs journey to the place where he was: in the city of Jerusalem, or some town or village in Galilee, or by the side of the lake. We hear of a party of Greeks who came to Jerusalem on Palm Sunday, perhaps having travelled a long way, and they asked to see Jesus.

So too, in the days after the Resurrection, Jesus made himself known visibly to the disciples, whether in a room in the city, or on the road to Emmaus, or by the Sea of Galilee.

But, with the final parting at the Ascension, the old way of his presence ended, and a new way began. Through his Holy Spirit Jesus was just as truly with his disciples, without their seeing him, and with no limits of space or time.

Where two or more meet together in his name, he will be there. When a Christian is alone in a prison cell, he will be there. In the sacrament of the Eucharist, he will be there: "Jesus, whom not having seen, you love".

A LOVELY AND TERRIBLE PRIVILEGE   January 6

To be a Christian at all is a privilege lovely and terrible enough; for a Christian is a brother of Christ, a member of Christ, with an intimate access to the very heart of God when he says, "Our Father" in Christ's name.

GO IN PEACE   January 7

What were some of the effects that Christ first had upon those who encountered him? There were some who felt very guilty on account of their sins, and he brought to them the assurance of forgiveness that lifted a load off their hearts when he said, "Go in peace and sin no more". And if that is you, if you are burdened with a feeling of guilt, be very sure that the absolution that Christ brings (that is, if you confess your sins and ask his forgiveness) can be real and overwhelming.

And then there were those, alas, who didn't realise their sinfulness because they were just complacent about themselves. And his grace brought home to them the real state of their need so that they could see themselves in the sight of God, and not just in the sight of their friendly and congratulating neighbours. And if that is you, and perhaps it is, be very sure that the grace of Christ can bring to you a sense of what you really are in the sight of God's love and righteousness, and re-beget in you a real contrition for your sinfulness, and a longing for his pardon.

IN THE TOTAL CONTEXT OF LIFE   January 8

The real Jesus appeals to a man in the total context of his life. No man lives in a vacuum. Every man is himself a complex of human relationships: he may be a father, a brother, a husband, a citizen of a town or country; he has a profession; he employs others or is employed by others; he has his politics, his amusements, his many human involvements. And the real Jesus does not convert a man as a "soul" to be "saved" in a vacuum, but as a person in the totality of his human relations.

It is indeed utterly wrong to bypass the need for personal conversion to Jesus, and to substitute for it a gospel of social action or human betterment. The real Jesus demands nothing less than the conversion of *you* in all those relationships whereby you are really and fully you.

The "hypocrisy" for which Jesus denounced the Pharisees so trenchantly did not mean insincerity: the Pharisees were very sincere in their religion and in their moral conscientiousness. Rather was that hypocrisy the wearing of blinkers, the blinkers in which we can think we are serving Jesus without noticing some urgent aspect of our service of him which is just around the corner—for instance, our attitudes and actions about race or poverty.

"WHERE I AM, THERE SHALL MY SERVANT BE ALSO"

January 9

At the present time there are many in this country and elsewhere who are calling on the name of Jesus, enrolling themselves in his

18

allegiance, sometimes in old-fashioned and familiar ways, sometimes in ways which may shock and outrage those who think they know better and pride themselves on the correctness of their faith.

It must have been like that on the day Jesus rode into Jerusalem on the ass's colt, and (as one of the evangelists tells us) "the whole city was stirred saying, who is this?" There would be those whose devotion was a shallow, excited curiosity. There would be those who tried to bring Jesus down to the level of their own emotions. There would be those who saw Jesus hopefully as the leader of their own political causes. And no doubt there were those to whom he was a kind of Jesus Christ Superstar. How disapproving his disciples would be. Certain that they knew better, and saying smugly, "This is not our Jesus".

But Jesus repels none who approach him, and sometimes, in the midst of what seems blasphemous and crude, there can be flashes of insight. Jesus exposes himself to the people, and rebukes those who would fend them off. But for those who begin to know him he has one answer, and we see it in the story of the Greek who approached with the request "Sir, we would see Jesus".

They put the request to Philip, and Philip passes it on to Andrew, and when it reaches Jesus his answer comes at once. "Truly, truly I say to you, unless a grain of wheat falls into the earth and dies, it stays by itself alone; but if it dies it bears much fruit. . . . If anyone serves me, he must follow me; and where I am, there shall my servant be also. If any man serves me, the Father will honour him."

THE JOURNEY TO THE FATHER   January 10

The life of Christ on earth is described by St. John as being all the way a journey to the Father. "I go to the Father." The words are a haunting refrain through the story as he goes his way to the Father, the lifting-up, the glory.

But the journey to the Father was at every moment a journey

deeper and deeper into humanity, with its sin, its sorrow, its death. And nowhere was Jesus more utterly in the Father's glory than when, in bearing the world's darkness and dereliction on Calvary, he cried out that he was bereft of God. Towards heaven, towards the world's darkness: these were two facets of one journey and one Christ. (SS)

THE BODY OF CHRIST   January 11

"Ye are the Body of Christ," St. Paul says to the Christians of his own day, and the words are still true: truly addressed to us who are Christians today.

"Ye are the Body of Christ," the family fellowship of those who with Christ and in Christ and through Christ are called to worship God in depth, and who by their worship are proclaiming the priority of God in the world.

They are called to carry the message of divine love brought by Christ to the world, and to serve humanity in the name of Christ. And that body of Christ, that society, is composed of the divine fact of Christ's forgiveness and Christ's life – "Peace be unto you" – and also by the human fact of horribly, horribly fallible and weak Christian men and women.

"YE ARE THE BODY OF CHRIST"   January 12

I was in a university and some of the Christian students were telling me about a superb effort that some of them were making to run a plan in their great city to enable the better housing of quite a number of its citizens. A wonderful piece of practical Christian work! Yet one of them said to me rather angrily, "Yes, we are doing this, but why doesn't the Church do something about it?"

Well, God bless my soul! "Ye are the Body of Christ," I had to tell these dear people. "Ye are the Body of Christ. It is the glory of the Church that you are doing that."

What they really meant by "Why doesn't the Church do something?" was "Why don't you, the Archbishop of Canterbury, pay attention and make a speech about it?" As if that can do any good to anybody at all! "Ye are the Body of Christ," and there, in that city, were those Christian students—they were not pagans, they were baptised Christians saying their prayers—living by the life of Christ and his Holy Spirit, doing this great piece of service, really being the Body of Christ.

THE CHRISTIAN CHURCH   January 13

In the midst of the world there is the Christian Church, the pledged followers of Jesus Christ, filled with Christ's own Spirit; the family and the community, not of those who are perfect, not always of those who are very good specimens of holiness, but of men and women and children who, by being pledged to Jesus crucified and risen, are being put into the way of being made holy, put into the discipline of that cleansing and sanctifying and perfecting which is the restoration of the true divine life in humanity.

THE FELLOWSHIP   January 14

The word *church* probably suggests to most people a kind of building. We talk about "going to church". But the original meaning of the word—and its basic meaning still—is different. It means people, the Christian people, the fellowship of those who adhere to Jesus Christ.

The earliest Christians didn't meet in great buildings like cathedrals: they met in one another's houses, or perhaps in the open air. They shared—as Christians everywhere will share—in a common belief expressed in the simple sentence *Jesus is Lord*. This meant the belief that Jesus is alive today, Jesus is divine, and Jesus claims lordship, sovereignty, over all human life.

The members of the Church were, and are, pledged to a way of life—unselfishness, brotherhood, mutual forgiveness, compassion, justice. How does one join? By baptism. The converts used to be brought to a stream or river, and after professing their belief that Jesus is Lord they would plunge under the water and step out into a new life—the Christian life.

How were the members held together with Jesus and with one another? Every week there is the sacrament of the Lord's Supper, also called the Holy Communion or the Eucharist. In this symbolic rite with bread and wine the Christians feed upon Christ's own life, receive him into their lives, and are joined closely to one another.

THE FORGIVEN MAN   January 16

The secret of the Christian is not that he is always in the right and puts other people in the right, but that he is a forgiven man. That is the secret of a Christian's humility, and his liberation to love God and his fellows with a new impulse.

So the strength of the Church is not the strength of its members, but the strength of Christ who forgives them, humbles them, and can do something with them. So no one is excluded who is ready to say, "I am sorry. God help me, a sinner".

In the final crisis all that St. Peter could say was "I am sorry", and Christ made him the rock man of the Church.

THE FAMILY OF THE FORGIVEN   January 17

The Christian Church has always both a divine element and a human element. It is divine because the risen Christ is with it. And when the members respond to this, Christ's power does produce wonderful lives, saintly and Christlike. We have all of us met such people.

But the Church has also its human element, because its members are made out of fallible human nature, which can often fail. So we see in history how the Church has times of compromise, or worldliness, or decline. Then sometimes after a period of decline God raises up a faithful remnant, and there come renewal and revival. Always the secret is God's forgiveness, and this is always man's chief need. Nothing is more false and tragic than the idea that our human race can climb by its own power to morality, brotherhood, or justice.

No, forgiveness is the great need, and forgiveness is the source of a new humility and love and compassion. The Church, as the family of forgiven men and women, exists to hold up this supreme need to the human race. Every one of its members can share in this work.

THREE SORTS OF CHRISTIAN   January 18

Probably there have always been three sorts of Christian. There are those who really respond to their calling, and there is something genuinely Christlike in their lives. There are those who are just formal, or conventional, or insincere, and they are the passengers in the boat. There is also the large number of struggling Christians who often fail, and they are grieved at their failure, but they press on, trusting to God's forgiveness. And in spite of their failures, they do help their fellows by pointing to the goal and not losing the vision of it.

EMOTION, WILL, IMAGINATION AND MIND   January 19

Jesus appealed and appeals to all the faculties of a person, not only to the emotions, but to the will and the imagination and the mind, too. Inevitably he appeals to the emotions, but he brings the love of God to bear upon the hearts and minds of people, and in that love he loves them himself utterly.

There can be no love without emotion, and in evoking love from those who know him, hearts are stirred. Emotion is certainly there, but the appeal to the will is there too. "Why call me Lord, Lord, and not do the things which I command?" If a man wills to do the will he shall know the doctrine whether it be of God. There's no knowledge of Jesus then or now apart from practical obedience when his will is discerned.

THINK IT OUT   January 20

Then there is the appeal of Jesus to the imagination, to the sense of wonder. How often we read in the gospel story that the people wondered at what Jesus did and said! They marvelled—the wondering imagination.

Jesus evokes that sense of wonder, and isn't it perhaps that sense of wonder which is a large part of what we call worship, and which really makes the difference between what is only an ethical allegiance, and what is religion?

And, too, Jesus appeals to the mind. Again and again he challenges his hearers to think. He doesn't reveal the truth to them in a kind of tabloid packet to be swallowed whole—"Shut your eyes and swallow". No, Jesus challenges his hearers, sowing seeds of truth in their minds and consciences, and then urging them to think out the meaning of it.

Think it out, think it out. It is in this process of thinking it out—together with the love and the will and the imagination—that Jesus and his message are made known.

EVERY SINGLE PERSON MATTERS   January 21

The individual man, woman, and child has eternal and everlasting value. Every single human person matters. He or she matters because God created that person, loves that person, and wants that person to be with him eternally in the closest loving fellowship.

Eternity proclaims the eternal infinite worth of every single person.

Because love is one and indivisible, the same love that draws us towards heaven with the ambition of heaven as our goal is the same love that sends us into the heart of the world where there is suffering, and hardship, and poverty, and distress. It sends us to be loving, and to serve our fellows.

The more we love and serve our fellows here, the nearer we are to heaven.

Our service in Christ's name to those who suffer is not something that we do to try to advertise Christianity as a good, useful public show. Our service to people who suffer is just a natural outflowing of our love of God, of our love of others: "For he who does not love his brother whom he has seen, how can he love God whom he has not seen?"

There are in our own country people who suffer very greatly. There are, for instance, those who are homeless, and those who are lonely. In other parts of what is now a very small and close-knit world there are people who suffer terribly through acute poverty, and actual hunger and starvation. Every Christian congregation should, as a true part of Christian discipleship, be setting itself deliberately to the task of helping and caring for those who suffer.

A baby "matters" more than a million stars, more than the process of evolution which led up to there being babies at all. He matters because he will presently be able to respond with reverence and love to *That* which gives meaning to the whole.

His response defines his duty in life, but involves what is in turn meaningless apart from the destiny beyond it. And if the *That* to which he responds is akin to what is significant in himself, then he may name his goal not *That* but *He*. (CP)

The unkindness of man to man is the heartbreaking tragedy of human history. It is always due to selfish and arbitrary likes and dislikes: liking this sort of man and disliking another sort of man because his character, or his opinions, or his race, or his religion are different, or because he stands in the way of one's own interests. And the unkindness of man to man has woven itself into the world's system.

A voice today is crying, "Turn back, O man, forswear thy foolish ways". But if this is to happen, man anywhere and everywhere must recognise that the other man is, like himself, made in God's own image after God's own likeness.

STREAM OF GOODNESS January 26

God's purpose is like a stream of goodness flowing out into the world and all its needs. But it is our privilege as God's children to help this stream of goodness to reach other people, becoming ourselves like channels. Our good actions can be channels of God's goodness, and so too can our prayers.

We do not bombard God with our desires; no, we bring our desires into tune with his, so that he, waiting upon our co-operation, and using the channel of our prayers, brings the stream of his good purpose into the parched deserts of human need. (MP)

OUR FATHER: THE MODEL PRAYER January 27

Jesus meant not only "pray in these words", but "pray with this sequence of thought and desire". God first, the Father, the heavenly Father, "hallowed be thy name". His name is his character and glory, to be dwelt upon, honoured, loved, our hearts and minds to be soaked in it. And *then* we ask that his reign may come and his will be done. With our wills first surrendered to his, we bring the affairs of the world to him in our requests. (MP)

Compassion in the care for humanity, integrity in the service of truth, contemplation of God in the stillness of prayer—may God give these gifts to his Church and to every one of its members. Serve humanity, reverence truth, contemplate your Creator. In doing the last of these, which is the first as well as last, the Psalmist says, "I will give thanks unto thee, for I am fearfully and wonderfully made".

Fearfully and wonderfully: these two adverbs tell us the heart of the matter; it is in awe and wonder that the knowledge of God comes—call it religion, or call it what you will. Fearfully and wonderfully: such is the way of God's approach to us, and such is the way of our response to him, who fearfully and wonderfully made us so that, through the selfless love of him and our fellow creatures, we should come to the vision of him as he is. (BR)

THE DOOR   January 29

The door of prayer towards heaven, towards the heart of God, is always a door of love into the world of human needs. (CP)

THE MEANING OF IT ALL   January 30

The goal of the relationship between you and God and God and you is "heaven". I want to suggest that you do not think about heaven as much and as often as you ought to, and that we of the clergy don't preach and teach about it nearly as much as we ought to. Because heaven is not a sort of very, very far away sort of last chapter of Christianity that we need not start bothering about quite just yet. No, *heaven is the meaning of it all.*

Heaven is simply the coming perfection of that fellowship between you and a God who made you, a God who loves you infinitely, a God who loves you so much that he cannot live a day without you, and who wants you with him everlastingly.

Beautifully does St. Augustine describe the goal of heaven: "We shall rest and we shall see, we shall see and we shall love, we shall love and we shall praise".

We shall rest—cease from our self-important busy-ness, acknowledging that what God does is infinitely significant, and that what we do signifies so little. We shall rest and, resting, our eyes shall be opened to the beginning of the vision of God himself. And "we shall see" leads on to "we shall love", for, seeing him, how shall we fail to love him with the fullness of affection and love? And love not only him but all the fellow-creatures destined to share heaven with him and with us—a perfection of the love and service of man for man in the sight and eyes of the Creator. We shall love perfectly, and we shall know that all flows from him, God the Perfect One. And so the final word will be praise. We shall rest, we shall see, we shall love, and we shall praise.

It will be the everlasting adventure of exploring all the depths of the infinite beauty and goodness: endless rest, and yet endless search and adventure. And that is heaven. Our existence here is but a brief prelude to it, and our thinking about it will make all the difference to what we are doing this day and this hour. Yet this day and this hour we are set here in this world, and God created this world as well as us, and we are part of this world—we are ourselves a portion of created nature.

And because love is indivisible, the love whereby we walk towards heaven as our goal is inseparable from the love whereby here and now we serve our fellows and care for everything in the world— because the world is God's.

FEBRUARY

THE SHAKING OF THE EARTH   February 1

The voice of God shook the earth when the divine law was given on Mount Sinai, a divine law which, reinterpreted by our Lord, still stands and must be proclaimed.

In the new covenant the voice of God shakes heaven as well as earth, for the Incarnation at Bethlehem and the Resurrection from the tomb belong to both earth and heaven.

Today the earth is being shaken and many things are cracking, melting, disappearing, and it is for us who are Christians to distinguish the things which are shaken, and to receive gratefully a kingdom which is not shaken: the kingdom of our crucified Lord. Within this kingdom we offer to God the worship he can accept. But as we do so we are never in cosy security: we have awe in our hearts for we are near to our God, and our God is a blazing fire.

THE MAN WHO HAS A LONGING   February 2

There is the man who has a longing, and a sense of void. "I cannot find God." "I cannot be sure of God." He has this emptiness, and this longing. But he clings on. He cannot relax. Sincerity about himself makes him thus grope for something beyond himself, though it all seems very dark.

My wish for such a man would not be that he should alter his state for another, but that he should find that his state has been indeed the rudiment of faith. In the history of Christianity there have been those who have known God in the warmth of conscious possession. There have also been those whose relation to God has long been a desire, an inability to let go, but all as in the thickness of a cloud. If you are like that, God—who is indeed deep mystery—may be finding you. There is an old prayer, "Before I sought thee, thou didst find me".

GIVE GOD A CHANCE   February 3

There is the man who has felt himself drawn towards the awareness of God and the serious consideration of the claim of Christ. But perhaps it is a passing awareness, a passing consideration among so many things that are exciting and interesting.

If you are that man, I beg you, allow yourself freedom to give this awareness a chance. You can easily lose that freedom the moment the pressures of your multiple life recur. To keep that freedom, quietness is needed—every day—deliberate, regular, protected; quietness to recollect that you have been aware of God and his claims. In that quietness you renew your desire towards God. "O my God, I want you. O my God, I thank you that I do want you. Give me freedom to want you more."

YOU CANNOT BY-PASS THE CHURCH   February 4

To be a Christian does not mean being "on the side of" Christianity, like one who supports a movement or approves of a cause. It means the submission of self to Christ, and the sharing in the life of his family.

Christ is the vine, and you are one of the branches. Holy Communion, and Prayer, and the Bible are ways in which Christ can keep you united to him; and these are wonderful gifts, involving stupendous demands. You cannot by-pass the Church: you are part of its scandal, unless you are setting yourself to be part of its glory.

"ONLY LOOK ON US AS FOUND IN HIM"   February 5
Our work should be done as well as possible as we share in the longing of Christ's own heart that *all* shall be saved.

But because our motive is Christ's longing and not our own ambition, we keep our moods of exaltation and of depression as near to him as we can. Our disappointments are thus turned into a means of sharing *his* grief: "Jesus beheld the city and wept over it". Our success moments are turning into a sharing in *his* joy: "Jesus rejoiced in the Holy Spirit and said, I thank thee, Father . . . that thou hast revealed these things unto babes".

Thus we can be schooled into something of the mind of our Lord about success and failure, something of the spirit of "and only look on us as found in him". When we are disappointed—it will be *his* grief. When we do "well"—it will be *his* joy. If it is our privilege to help and serve only one single soul in his name, that is more than we deserve, for we know that to God the worth is infinite.

THEOLOGY IS ABOUT PEOPLE   February 6
F. D. Maurice knew better than many of his contemporaries that Christian truth is about every man and woman and child. Theology is about them, or it is not about God at all. (CP)

A TALE OF UPS AND DOWNS   February 7
All our ideas of success and failure are turned upside down by a look at our Lord's ministry, his training of the apostles, and the

final issue of his work. What were the successes? The crowds who thronged him for comfort and healing? Or a talk with one woman of Samaria by the well? Or a talk with one Nicodemus in the night? What do we make, in terms of success and failure, of the scene at the end of the sixth chapter of St. John when, after some hard teaching, "many of the disciples walked no more with him"? What of the Crucifixion? It is well to put all our success talk in the lights and shades of the gospel story.

So too in the history of the Church. It has fallen to some of God's servants to lead many souls into the Church's fellowship. It has fallen to others to sow some seeds with no apparent result, and the reaping has been for another generation. It has fallen to others to help a few people greatly, and it is not unlike our Lord to give infinite care to individuals here and there.

And work which seems sad and frustrated? There are things which God can do with it. The history of the Kingdom of God on earth is no steady development, but a tale of ups and downs, victories and reverses. But the pieces are in God's hands.

BONHOEFFER   February 8

When I am confronted by someone who is on any showing a genuine Christian thinker, and a man very near to God in the way of martyrdom, I think it right to learn all I can from him. And what I learn from Bonhoeffer's *Letters from Prison* is this.

First, that God can be found within the heart of the world's tragedy, far outside the religious camp or the sphere of religious practice.

Secondly, that for all that Bonhoeffer says about "religionless Christianity", there is religion growing powerfully in his own soul in the days and hours of his imprisonment. Many of the letters show him drawing upon psalms, hymns, the memory of festival and fast, prayers written and spoken, the rhythms of word and thought which are the stuff of Christian tradition. There grows in him that submissiveness which in his critique he names as the characteristic of religion—but in him it is not childish but childlike (the difference is profound), and not retrogressive but growing in strength as it passes beyond the words of liturgy into the silence of contemplation. Through psalms, hymns, and spiritual songs this man of faith, this child of God, passes into the realm of "Be still and know that I am God". If I am sceptical about Bonhoeffer's criticism of religion as a thing belonging to man's immaturity it is because he himself shows the power of religion in depth; and he shows it not as something regressive, but as something which moves forward from strength to strength. We are reminded of what some mystical writers of old called "the terrible strength of the saints".

Truly Bonhoeffer's God is not the God of religion in the limiting sense. He is the living God, found amidst the desolation as indeed the God of Jesus was found deep in the desolation of Calvary. But when God is found, a man is unlikely to be silent: words come to his heart and lips. And, if he is a Christian, the words may be his own and in part those which link him with the fellowship of saints all through the ages, till words yield to the silent contemplation of the Creator. (BR)

HUMAN RIGHT   February 9

Here indeed is a human right which no cruelty in the world can snatch from any man, the right to be loved by God, the right to respond to that love and to reach the destiny.

A man can rob himself of his heavenly goal by his own stubbornness. But others cannot rob him of it. However his fellows may treat him by cruelty or persecution, they cannot snatch from him his right to live with God for ever. God will be his portion and his joy.

LET US PRAY FOR THEM   February 10

Our heart goes out to those in prison, without justice, because of their opinions, or because of their religion or their dissent from

33

the regime under which they live. Our heart goes out to those who are separated from their fellows, or denied equal citizenship or a citizen's privileges because their skins are of a certain colour. Our heart goes out to those whom our world's economic failure condemns to poverty and hunger. Our heart goes out to all of these.

We pray for them and their families, and for those who injure them.

THE WAY, THE TRUTH, AND THE LIFE   February 11

We who are Christians are living in exciting times. While the old institutional Churches are under the weather and often looked at askance, the name of Jesus is making a great appeal.

Often those who are stirred by the name of Jesus may miss important parts of the truth about him, but we can be sure that he rejects none who try to find him. It is in the scriptures that Jesus is made known in all his claims as the way, the truth, and the life.

EXCITING DAYS LIE AHEAD   February 12

Not surprisingly, many young Christians are critical of the old institutional Churches, and look for Christian fellowship and mission in new ways outside the old Church structures.

These developments are sometimes called experimental Christianity, in contrast with the institutional Christianity of the past. The spirit of Christ blows and inspires in lots of ways, sometimes inside the old Churches, and sometimes outside them. And in the coming days we shall need to try to draw together not only Catholics and Protestants, but also the older Churches on the one hand, and the new experimental forms of Christianity on the other.

Exciting days lie ahead of all of us who try to be Christians. Both Christianity and the Church are dynamic, and indeed, explosive realities.

For Jesus Christ is with us still.

34

At times in the Church's history there has been far too much of a false kind of withdrawal and apartness: a withdrawal into religious pietism away from the hard facts of life amongst which the Church has to minister.

Now, in contrast, the call is to get away from pietism and to plunge our ministry right into the heart of the secular world around us. And, entirely rightly, we are urged to identify ourselves with the lives of the people, and to find the presence of God not in religion but in everyday circumstances.

And of course how right that is. It is part of the message of the Transfiguration that God is to be found in life's daily circumstances, and life's daily circumstances are to be transformed. But yet we may have nothing of Christ, nothing of God, and nothing of the supernatural to bring to the contemporary world unless we have—under the orders of Jesus—our own times of quiet and withdrawal and contemplation. And when we do that, we do it for the sake of the people just as Jesus, in his own withdrawal, was doing it for the sake of the disciples and for the sake of the world.

NEW TIMES, NEW WAYS   February 14

It is plainly right for churchmen to examine their methods and techniques again and again. It is wrong to stick to old ways of doing things in the face of experience that newer ways answer better to our times.

It is no less wrong to suppose that the newest ways will be of any avail without depth of prayer and love, and without width of human sympathy.

THE CREDIBLE CHURCH   February 15

It is more and more apparent that Christians are incredible unless they stand with the underprivileged in the world, and that the

Church is incredible if it is not clearly on the side of justice in the world's conflicts. This is behind the powerful swing towards Christian social and political activism, and I have mentioned the deep theological root which such activism can have.

Yet the Church is called to resist the temptation to justify itself by its political and social works, remembering how the Messiah resisted a like temptation in the wilderness when he said "no" to the idea of using either bread or power to win the world to God. Thus the Church's energies for the world's re-creation are to be rooted in the Church's message of reconciliation to God, and the Church's power of being the soul of the world is linked with its other-worldly calling, witnessing to heaven as man's true home. (CP)

TO SHARE IN THE SUFFERING   February 16

We cannot honourably commend to other people idealistic Christian actions which we ourselves are unwilling to practise or share. This error can take two forms. We can encourage people to belligerence while ourselves keeping out of the conflict, or we can say to other people that of course their Christian calling is to suffer patiently in the spirit of the Cross of Christ.

In either case we can safely say anything at all only if we are ready to be one with those who are suffering. It is this that is imperative: it is also this that is sometimes so hard as to be nearly impossible. That is our tragic situation. (CP)

THE POWER OF CHOICE   February 17

If my God is righteous and loving, how can my faith stand up to the appalling mess that there is in the world: the wrongdoing, the injustice, the terrible suffering?

God, loving and righteous, made the human race a race of moral beings who are able, with his help, to become loving and righteous like him, and to mould the world accordingly. But a moral being must have free will, a power of choice. Without that power of choice there is no freedom, morality, or love: free will is the condition of a moral universe. And a vast amount of the suffering and injustice in the world is caused by the wills of human beings acting as individuals, or as groups or nations, with such selfishness, fear, and lack of sensitivity that the flood of suffering has ensued.

My faith in God looks at the world and sees the world under judgment. And by the world under judgment I don't mean that God sends arbitrary punishment for wrongdoing. I mean that there is an inexorable moral law that wrongdoing brings its own consequences. My faith then says that we must turn to God and live as he would have us live.

THE UNCOMPROMISING GOAL   February 18

The ideal that every human being has set before him is the ideal of utter goodness, of holiness, of perfection. You and I are here not just to muddle through life, being fairly good, or rather good, or making a fairly good show of our existence in this world. No, we are created by God in order to come one day to share in God's own perfection of love and righteousness, of purity and unselfishness. And it is only by having that uncompromising goal before us that we are likely to be effective in loving and serving our fellows in the here and now.

Eternity portrays the uncompromising perfection of the goal for each one of us: the ideal that is nothing less than God-likeness.

NOTHING GOOD IS EVER WASTED   February 19

No act of goodness, heroism, or self-sacrifice performed in this world, however unsuccessful the result may seem to be, is ever lost or wasted. How often there are in human life acts of heroism and really sacrificial love, and the result seems to be nothing! The cause

37

seems to be lost. But because God has put eternity into man's mind, we know that nothing good or worthy is ever lost. It has an eternal value, and God can use it in ways beyond our knowledge and understanding in his good and great purpose for the coming of his kingdom.

Now, that gives us a new perspective to our present human struggle for righteousness. No righteous act is ever really lost, however fruitless it may at the moment seem to be, because God takes it up into an eternal purpose beyond our seeing, our dreaming, and indeed beyond this visible world.

HE WANTS UNIQUE YOU   February 20

Each of us is created in God's own image, and it means that, though we are creatures and full of sins and defects, there is a deep-down likeness between us and God, and our destiny is to be with him. When we say that God loves us we mean that he cares for each single one of us as if there is no one else for him to care for.

He cares for you in all that unique individuality which is yours. He wants *you* to be with him for ever, to share with you all that he has to share.

That is heaven. It is the perfection of the God-and-man relationship. And it cannot be selfish in any way because it implies the plural, and heaven includes the mutual love and service of all who share it together: a love and service totally integrated with the love of God and the vision of God. (MP)

THE MARK OF A SAINT   February 21

It is not being *virtuous* that makes a saint: the Pharisees were very virtuous, and they and their virtues needed conversion. It is not *doing good* in the world that makes a saint; he often does do good, but so do many people whom we would never call saints. It is

38

not the practice of *religion* which makes a saint. I expect you and I are pretty religious, but our religion, like every part of us, needs converting. No, the saint is one who has a strange nearness to God and makes God real and near to other people.

A saint embodies the parable of the corn of wheat that falls into the earth and dies. His virtues do not make him proud, for he is reaching out towards a perfection far beyond them and is humbled by the quest. His sins and failings, which may be many and bitter, do not cast him down, for the divine forgiveness humbles him and humbles him again. He shares and bears the griefs of his fellows, and he feels the world's pains with a heightened sensitivity; but with that sensitivity he has an inner serenity of an unearthly kind which brings peace and healing to other people.

This strange blending of humility, sorrow, and joy is the mark of a saint, and through him God is real and near. (CP)

THE PROBLEM OF GOOD   February 22

My faith in God is most acutely tested by the existence of suffering which seems to have no special wrongdoing at base. Indeed, belief that God is almighty and all-loving is strained for the sensitive Christian until he goes on to see the divine way of dealing with suffering in the Cross of Christ. There the answer comes.

But it is an answer which is not speculative, but practical, for it is an answer that is valid only when something like the spirit of Christ has been translated into human lives—lives which show what can be made of human suffering in terms of heroic saintliness. Such lives are faith's most powerful witnesses, for just when the problem of evil oppresses us they assault us with the problem of good. Faith is a costly thing, valid only in terms of the challenge to a costly way of life. Those who possess it have found it to be not an escape from life's conflicts, but a way of meeting those conflicts with the certainty that the power of God and of goodness will prevail.

What the Church teaches about the imitation of Christ, about prayer, about watchfulness, about the Church and its ministry and authority, about the scriptures, about Eucharist and worship, about the Holy Spirit, about the glory of God, about the judgment of nations, all has its significance in the light of the Passion, and in that light it is to be learned and taught. None of these theories distracts from the cardinal gospel that Jesus died for our sins according to the scriptures; they illuminate it and are illuminated by it.

That gospel will be shown both as one of victory, as St. John presented it, and one of tenderness and compassion, as St. Luke presented it, but never without the awe and loneliness with which St. Mark first described it. The Church which faces that awe will grasp more clearly the compassion and the victory: its power to be Lucan and Johannine will spring from the depth of its Marcan experience.

In its faithfulness to the whole treasure which the Passion narratives convey to it, the Church will be watchful and not sleeping, watchful not to miss what the narratives can bring to the mind and the conscience, not to miss what the Lord may say and do in the contemporary hour. By concerning himself with the narratives of the Passion a Christian puts himself in a place of terrible danger, lest at any time the Lord may come and find him sleeping.

LOVELY AND BEYOND   February 24

God's created world is lovely, but it is nothing to what is beyond. And what is beyond is already near and within, the meaning of the Christian's present union by faith with his Lord. So, "We look not at the things which are seen, but at the things which are not seen: for the things which are seen are temporal, but the things which are not seen are eternal". (SS)

God is the friend of man, and in any exchange between God and man God will be the one who is giving far more, giving so much that what man gives seems feeble, tiny, almost nothing. It is God who searches, finds, gives, and what he gives is *himself*. That is the meaning of Christmas, Good Friday, Easter—God giving himself in generous self-giving to mankind, so that he is near us, with us, in us, in ways beyond our imagining.

God and us; yes, God and us together, and together in wonderful nearness. And when we pray we shall not be bombarding God with our own desires. We shall be starting far nearer to God, sharing a little of his heart and mind, and putting our will at his disposal to serve his good purpose in the world. (MP)

How do we co-operate with God's good purpose towards the world? Partly by our actions, which are a channel of God's purpose, and partly by our prayers, which are also a channel of God's purpose. And while there are some who are called almost entirely to serve the world by prayer, and there are some whose activities are so tremendous that in actual time their prayers may be short, most of us—unless we know otherwise—are called to be channels of God's purpose in the world in both our actions and our prayers.

And we best do it if we first and foremost put ourselves in touch with the great stream of God's loving purpose and become channels in his name, irrigating the parched desert of a world saddened, divided, sinful and estranged.

While we thus pray and enjoy the presence of God, we remember the world around us with its terrible divisions, sins, sadnesses, needs and frustrations. And we remember our own terrible sins and needs and frustrations because we are part of the miserable world around us. So we intercede; and when we intercede, what do we really do? ... I think this is what we do. We don't start with the world and its needs; we don't start with ourselves and our ideas about the world's needs; we start as far as we can with God, and with God's loving purpose.

The key to intercession is to start by putting ourselves in line with God and his love and his purpose as far as we possibly can. We can think of God's attitude towards the world as one which loves it utterly; is full of goodwill, care, and beneficence; whose love thrusts towards the world like a great stream.

But, because God created the human race in his own image, God in his dealing with the world waits upon the co-operation of human wills in his beneficent purpose towards the world. It is very mysterious, but that is so; it is just a part of the dignity of the human race as free beings in God's own image that it is through them and through their co-operation that God designs his good things for the world.

THE SPUR TO PRESS ON   February 28

As long as we are a human race that is sinful and selfish, it is hard to see how we would ever learn to leave off being selfish and sinful if we lived in a world that was uniformly smooth and comfortable, without catastrophes and without accidents. In such a world there would be no spur whatever to us to be pressing on through virtue—especially through heroic virtue—towards a world beyond this. Perhaps the existence of the phenomenon of suffering in the world is not only a spur to courageous brotherhood between man and man, but also the spur to press on to the goal of another world altogether. And it was of another world that the apostle spoke when he wrote, "The sufferings of the present time are not worthy to be compared with the glory that shall be revealed".

We are sometimes rather shy of thinking about heaven and talking about the goal of heaven, because critics of Christianity are in the habit of telling us that the idea of heaven is a sort of selfish compensation dragged in to try to compensate ourselves for the frustrations of the world. But because heaven is a state of total unselfish perfect love, no selfish motive and no selfish action can get us one step nearer to heaven. And heaven isn't a selfish compensation for the frustrations of this world. Heaven is the glorious climax of the sacrificial love which ought to be seen manifested in this world. Think of the most heroic acts of sacrifice and love which can be counted in this world—well, heaven is like that. Heaven is the consummation of that.

WHAT THE WORLD REALLY IS   February 29

To bring the world to Christ is to uncover what the world really is. (CP)

MARCH

COMMITMENT TO A WAY   March 1

Faith is an act of the whole person. It is a commitment of the self to a way of understanding experience, and a commitment of the self to a way of life.

And while this belief in God is not a discovery of our reason, and is not something which our reason can prove, it claims to be congruous with reason: congruous with my reason inasmuch as, without it, the sense I see in the world becomes nonsense; congruous with reason inasmuch as it gives a view of man and the world which makes rational sense of the world's most significant aspects.

SUPREME IN THE UNIVERSE   March 2

I think that the sense, deep in man, that love, goodness, self-sacrifice are the supreme things in the universe is the key to belief in God.

These supreme things demand a response. And what sort of response? Faced with the highest and the best that I know, my response will be *obedience* and *wonder*. We must *obey* the impulse to love and goodness, and obedience involves the will. There is a saying of Jesus, "If a man wills to do my will he shall know the doctrine". We get to know more about moral reality by obeying it. And *wonder*: we marvel at the heights of goodness and beauty, and wondering, marvelling, brings our imagination into play.

This sense of love, goodness, self-sacrifice as the purpose for man, calling for the obedient will and the wondering imagination, is the stuff of which belief in God is made.

THE PROCESS OF CREATION   March 3

The story in Genesis about God's creation is not a literal piece of history or science, but a marvellous parable of how the world depends utterly upon God, and how he made the world in its many stages or phases.

But of course the discoveries of modern science—geology, biology and the rest—have shown us more and more of what these marvellous successive stages in the process of divine creation are: the existence of inorganic matter, then the emergence of life, primitive animals, mammals, animals in which intelligence and consciousness appear. Then, at some undefinable point in the series, there comes man, man so marvellous—but perhaps man is not more marvellous than the marvel of what emerged at every single stage of the process.

But this is the drama of divine creation: the Spirit of God working in the world with man as climax, suggesting that the whole process is in order that man may emerge in his glory and his potentialities.

And what is there in this creative process about man that makes him so utterly different from the phenomena which have preceded him? There are lots of ways in which that might be analysed or described, but the Bible says, "God created man in his own image, after his own likeness".

The wonderful thing about man is that he is describable as being in God's own image. Not that God and man are identical in all respects—far from it. God remains the Creator, and we always remain creatures, utterly dependent upon him. Yet there is a true affinity between God and man. Man has powers of memory, thought, consciousness, purpose, appreciation of beauty, appreciation of truth, moral distinction between right and wrong, and a rare potentiality of freedom. Above all he has the possibility of really knowing God, and having fellowship with God.

AWE AND DEPENDENCE   March 4

It is the potentiality of knowing the Creator of the infinite universe and having fellowship with him that is man's marvel, though of course when we speak of man's fellowship with God, we remember that it is not the fellowship of equals, but a fellowship deeply shot through with awe and dependence.

The nearer we get to God in real intimate fellowship as the very friend of God, the more we are humbled by this awe and dependence, abasing ourselves in the very start of our friendship with him, and we do what the Bible calls "give glory to God".

The end of this intimacy between man and God—man made in God's image—is nothing less than heaven. Heaven is the crown and consummation of man's rightful destiny as created in the image of God.

THE FINALITY OF JESUS   March 5

We must never substitute incomplete Old Testament ideas about God, about theology, about the world, about social relationships, for the finality of Jesus. For now we know that God is Christ-like, and in him is no unChrist-likeness at all.

In the narrative of the Transfiguration, and in the picture of the Transfiguration which stands for all time, Moses and Elijah are there, and law and prophecy are still part of the Holy Scripture. They are still present for us, bearing lively witness to Jesus.

Law? Law still has its place: but Christianity is no legalism. The reign of the spirit supersedes the reign of law. Yet law has its place in the ordering of human lives under God. And we must never forget that.

A FOLLY AND A SCANDAL   March 6

The faith to which we are called will always be folly and scandal to the world. It cannot be—in the usual sense of the word—popular; it is a supernatural faith, and it cannot adapt itself to every passing fashion of human thought. But it will be a faith alert to distinguish what is shaken and is meant to go, and what is not shaken and is meant to remain.

When men today tell us that they revere Jesus but find God or theism without meaning, it is sometimes because the image of God we Christians present is the image of a God of religious concerns but not of compassion for all human life. It is just not recognisable as the God and Father of Jesus Christ. So too, when men reject theism, it sometimes means that they cannot accept, in this shaken world an easy facile assumption that the universe has a plan, a centre, a purpose.

It is for us Christians to be sure that our faith is no facile assumption, but a costly conviction that in Christ crucified and risen, in suffering and victorious love and in no other way, there is a plan, a centre, a purpose. In dying to live, in losing life so as to find it— there is the place where divine sovereignty is found, and theism has meaning and vindication.

MAN'S ROLE   March 7

It is in the middle of this world that man is set to worry out his duty towards his eternal Creator.

The classic description of man's role in the world in the Bible is in the eighth psalm: "O Lord our governor, how excellent is thy name in all the world. . . . What is man that thou art mindful of him?" And the psalmist goes on to say that man, though a humble creature, has been set above other creatures in the world in order to rule them and be lord over them—but only as God's viceroy, so to speak, because man, though he has a wonderful lordship and control over all the world of nature, must himself be subject to God if he is to exercise his control aright.

So man is meant to be serving God in the middle of all the world's phenomena. Man must sow seed, grow corn, get food, dig the mines, extract minerals, fish the seas, make sharp implements for agriculture and industry ... all of which leads on to village life and town life and city life, and civilisation and commerce and culture and economics and politics, and the whole of man's involvement in the things of the earth.

And what is it all for? It is that man may use this potential power of ruling and controlling the world, not for his own aggrandisement, not for lording it over his neighbour, not for strife between group and group, nation and nation, race and race, but in fellowship with his brethren, and all the time in humble dependence upon God the Creator.

Because it is when human beings are in humble dependence upon God that they discover that true purpose of fellowship with one another: serving one another and glorifying God, and using all the processes of civilisation for that great end. That is what we are really here for—fulfilling the purpose of our good and great God who is here in the heart of the world, and here in the heart of us, as well as beyond the world.

SOMETHING HAS GONE WRONG   March 8

But something has gone wrong. Something has gone most disastrously wrong, and Christian theology describes that something which has gone wrong as the Fall and Original Sin.

Believing in the fallenness of man does not turn upon believing literally in Adam and Eve. No, Adam and Eve are a splendid parable of what has gone wrong. Again, it does not mean that man was

49

originally perfect on earth, for we have no evidence of that at all. No, what it means is that in the very middle of man's development and progress and evolution there has come a sort of false twist of pride, self-sufficiency, self-satisfaction, self-will: man worshipping himself and pleasing himself instead of conscientiously and humbly following the path laid down by God the Creator.

Not only is biological evolution a reality, but so also is human progress, and man really does develop his mental power and his moral power, spiritually, morally, culturally. Yet, in the middle of it, there is this false twist of pride: pride—bumptious, self-satisfied independence, which is what we call Original Sin.

We know it in our own individual consciousness because when we get rather better, and grow a few virtues in our system, there is then the terrible liability to wreck it all by being proud and pleased with ourselves, and our last state may be no better than our first. The same thing happens in the story of civilisations—civilisations achieving wonders of moral power as well as scientific and intellectual power, and then wrecking themselves through this self-satisfaction issuing in pride, aggressiveness, greediness, quarrelsomeness, and materialism.

This truth of man's fallenness and Original Sin is written into our own personal self-awareness—at least, it is very bitterly so in mine, and I expect it is in yours. It is also bitterly written into our historical diagnosis of the story of human civilisation. What a world! What a mess! What division! What frustration! But it remains God's world, and somehow God is still in the heart of it, and the Spirit of God is ever striving with man, and does not cease to strive.

THE ANTICIPATION   March 9
But already—and this is the joy of Christianity—already there are anticipations of heaven set within our present existence.

Every prayer is an anticipation of heaven—for what is prayer essentially? It is the soul of the creature lifting itself up into touch with the Creator. So too, every act of truly selfless love between man and man is an anticipation of heaven where love will rule in perfection. So too is every act of contrition, of confession of sin, an anticipation of heaven. For when you confess your sins and seek absolution you are acknowledging that you are nothing, nobody but a sinner, and God is all and has the glory. It is just that acknowledgement by the penitent that makes the very act of penitence an anticipation of heaven. That is why the Lord says that the angels are rejoicing when we truly confess our sins.

GOD'S ANSWER   March 10

God the Creator answers the world's frustrations by giving himself to be the Rescuer and Saviour. Humanity fails to give itself rightly to humanity and to God; so God's answer is to give himself utterly to humanity. That is the meaning of Jesus Christ, and Calvary, and Easter.

"The Word became flesh and dwelt among us, and we beheld his glory, full of grace and truth." God was rescuing the world and humanity from the mess into which it had got itself.

WHAT SHALL WE DO?   March 11

Throughout Lent we pray that "we worthily lamenting our sins and acknowledging our wretchedness may obtain of thee, the God of all mercy, perfect remission and forgiveness". It is fine language and a fine sentiment: but if it is to be real we must do something practical about it. What shall we do? We must set about in a deliberate way to examine ourselves, to be sorry, to confess to God, to be sure of his forgiveness.

1. *Self-examination.* We do this best by not looking at ourselves in an introspective way, but by looking at our Lord Jesus Christ, with a glance at ourselves beside him. If we think first

of his love and goodness to us, there will quickly come to us a realisation of our ingratitude, pride and selfishness. Then we should go on to examine ourselves quite specifically; asking what are the particular things we have done, or left undone, and know to be against the will of God. When did you last make a self-examination that was quite definite and specific? I am sure the devil loves us to be vague about this.

2. *Sorrow.* This is the realisation that our sin has hurt our Lord. We try to grasp that our Lord's suffering in the Passion is the picture of how, ever and always, our sin is wounding to the love of God. Some feel this sorrow more easily than others, and we need to ask God to *make* us sorry, to help us to repent. "Lord, I am sorry for my sin. Help me to be more sorry by thy grace." The deliberate will to be sorry matters far more than keen feelings of sorrow.

3. *Confession.* How shall we confess our sins? In its wisdom, our Church gives us freedom either to confess them alone to God, or to confess them in the presence of a priest so as to receive from him God's word of absolution. The idea that "going to confession" is an issue of party controversy has almost entirely disappeared. The liberty not to use sacramental confession is recognised: so is the liberty to use it. Those who confess their sins in this way do something which is thorough, costly, decisive. Through the pain of the confession and the joy of absolution given by the priest in God's name, they are brought near to our Lord. Whichever way of confession we choose, we are *all* called to confess our sins to God with care and sincerity.

4. *Forgiveness.* We must first be ready to forgive all others. God's past forgiveness of us is the great incentive to our forgiveness of others, for his undeserved love towards ourselves cuts the ground beneath any claim we have to be harsh or unforgiving about others. God's forgiveness is called "absolution" because it is a setting free. But after receiving forgive-

ness, we must use the freedom to follow new resolutions. "I will run the way of thy commandments: because thou hast set my heart at liberty."

TOWARDS EASTER   March 12

An Easter faith which is true is always a faith which includes the wounds of Calvary. When Christ was raised from the dead, it did not mean that the Cross was left behind. Far from it. The risen Christ is always the Christ who was once crucified. Cross and Resurrection go together.

Christian imagery and Christian art have portrayed this through the centuries. We recall pictures of the Crucifixion which show the kingly triumph, the majestic peace already breaking through the scene of death. We recall pictures of the risen Jesus which show the marks of sacrifice never effaced, and carried into the risen glory. And the art and the imagery convey deep truth. We can never know the risen Jesus and never serve him unless we face the reality of the Cross.

We must still repent of the sins which wound him, as our sins always do. We must still find him in those who suffer as we go and serve him in them. Never can the notes of Calvary fade from the Church's songs of victory. (CP)

"THE HIDING PLACE OF GOD'S POWER"   March 13

Not only do the evangelists tell of the Passion as one unbroken story; they also tell of it with one dominant motif, and this despite the considerable differences between them in craftsmanship and theology. The motif is not the heroism of Jesus, nor the horror of the event. The appeal is not to sorrow, or pity, or admiration. Rather does the story dwell on how evil does its worst, and yet God overrules the evil for his great ends.

Human evil is at work, human evil which St. Luke and St. John

53

describe as directed by supernatural forces, and evil has Jesus in its power and carries him step by step to destruction. There is a terrible undertone in the verb παραδίδωμι as it tells of Jesus "handed over" by Judas to the Jews, by the Jews to Pilate, by Pilate to death. Evil has him in its grasp. Yet all the while God is at work executing his own majestic purpose—foretold in the scriptures—and mightily contriving to bring salvation through what happens.

In cruce latebat sola Deitas (Deity was hidden in the Cross), wrote St. Thomas Aquinas. "The cross was the hiding place of God's power," wrote Luther. Both phrases catch the spirit of the narratives of the Passion, not least the narrative of St. Mark. The response which the evangelists would evoke from their readers is faith—not primarily repentance, but primarily faith: the belief that here in the Crucifixion men stand in the presence of the divine.

DARKNESS AND GLORY   March 14

Jesus taught his disciples again and again that the ignominious death he was going to die was not going to be just one more tragedy added to the world's load of tragedies; no, tragic and painful though it was going to be, it was also going to be something used by God as a mighty divine act to give the divine answer to the sin and suffering of the world. His ignominious death was going to be something powerful, divine, majestic. And it happened so. Think of two of the accounts of the Passion on Good Friday.

The earliest account is St. Mark's, and you remember how he brings out the darkness and loneliness, and the desolation of it all. Jesus is utterly deserted. Jesus is plunged into total darkness, and from the depths of the darkness there comes the cry, "My God, my God, why hast thou forsaken me?" He saved others, himself he cannot save. Jesus just gives himself up utterly to share in the darkness of mankind, the darkness of the sinful and suffering human situation of death.

And now look at the other account—that in St. John. He tells the same story, the story of an ignominious death; and yet he tells the story with a kind of title above it, and a title beneath it, and indeed a title wrapped all round it: and that title is the word "glory". St. John shows that this terrible death was and is Christ's glory, divine glory, because it was total self-giving love. And total self-giving love was glory, Christ's glory, God's glory, the very glory of the essence of Godhead itself. What was a scene of lowly destruction is transformed through sacrifice into a scene of glory.

THE LAST SUPPER   March 15

On the night before his death Jesus made wise provision whereby his followers in subsequent generations could be united with him in the meaning of his death. This provision—the Eucharist, Holy Communion, Liturgy, Mass, Lord's Supper—was given not only for the centuries of man's immaturity and religion, but also for the rest of time "until his coming again".

This rite has through the centuries gathered around itself the poetry, art, music, ceremony, architecture, of successive Christian cultures. It has been loved and cherished as a "thing in itself", the feast which Jesus makes. But the meaning of the rite is pride humbled, hearts broken, as Christians face the suffering of Christ, and painfully and joyfully give themselves to the service of God and humanity. (SS)

THE BREAD, THE CUP, AND US   March 16

"Jesus, in the night in which he was betrayed, *took* bread . . . likewise after supper he *took* the cup." He takes the elements in his hands, and he does with them—to the Father's glory and for the feeding of men's souls—what is beyond our understanding.

So, too, Jesus takes *us*. That is the meaning of the call to holiness which the Eucharist implies from first to last. Jesus takes *us*.

Today is St. Patrick's Day. Thousands of Christian people in every part of the world will be remembering Ireland's saint and missionary. Let them not forget—let none of us forget—how it was that St. Patrick won people throughout Ireland, far and wide, to Christ and the Christian faith.

What was it in his character which marked him and gave him such power? History leaves us in no doubt. Patrick was a forgiving man, a man of reconciliation. As a youth he had been kidnapped and held in Ireland as a slave, and for some years he had suffered terribly. In the course of those years he became a Christian, and later, living on the Continent, he was called to be a missionary.

So he goes back to the people who had ill-used him. He will care for them, win them, serve them in Christ's name. "Who compelled me?" he asks. "I am a slave to Christ for the unspeakable glory of the eternal life that is in Christ our Lord."

A man of forgiveness, a reconciler: can we doubt that his prayers are with us today as we pray for a miracle of reconciliation? Miracle? Yes, that is what Christianity is about, a miracle in human relationships.

From a sermon in Westminster Roman Catholic Cathedral, 1972

BOUND TOGETHER   March 18

That none lives to himself and none dies to himself is an inescapable fact. The lives of men and women interlock, and their fortunes are bound together in a bundle. When they try to act as if this were not so, they injure themselves as well as their neighbours by violating a law of human existence.

What is true of men and women is true of nations. If we are to think of Europe as a unity, we must first notice the plain fact of the interrelation of its countries through the centuries. There is not one of them whose story can be told without frequent allusion to its debt—whether of gratitude or ingratitude—to its neighbours. No country has ever lived to itself, or ever can.

THE SECRET OF EUROPE   March 19
Within all the countries of Europe today, those who believe that Jesus Christ is Lord of the dead and the living and pledge themselves to accept his practical lordship are a minority of people. If there was once an equation between Christendom and Europe, that equation is untrue today. It is indeed still possible to point to the marks of past Christian tradition, to claim that our culture has powerful elements derived from Christianity, and to know that the great works of Christian literature, art and architecture stand for something in the present as well as in the past.

It would be wrong to belittle the diffused presence of Christian ideals. Yet this diffused presence has grown thin; and positive, convinced, passionate Christian conviction is shared by the few. But they, the practising Christians, Catholic or Protestant or Orthodox, hold a faith wherein the secret of Europe lies. They understand the Europe of the past in its glories and its failures, and they hold the key to the Europe of the future—for the key is Jesus Christ, Lord of the dead and the living.

MORE THAN EUROPEAN   March 20
The older Europe thought of itself—inaccurately and yet plausibly—as conterminous with Christendom. We who are Christians in Europe today are unlikely to forget that Christianity in Europe is but a small fraction of Christianity throughout the world.

On every continent Christianity is to be found. It is misleading to see it as a primarily European phenomenon. The Second Vatican Council reflected vividly the more-than-European character of the Roman Catholic Church. The Lambeth Conference of Anglican

57

bishops in 1968 reflected the more-than-European character of the Anglican Communion. Other Churches have had a like experience.

Christian leadership in the world arises from many countries and races. So the European Christianity of the future may not be the "leading" Christianity in the world. The Holy Catholic Church of the future will involve itself with many national cultures, but it will identify itself with none. (CP)

FORGET OURSELVES   March 21

The division of the world into countries which are well off and countries where poverty is acute constitutes a crisis for the world. What can we do?

Even though our own giving touches but the tiniest fraction of the need, our giving is the test of our personal concern. We do not hesitate to say that our Government must not diminish what it gives in real terms to overseas aid. And those who have the knowledge and skill in the well-to-do countries must find the economic policies which the world situation requires. Would that as a country we could leave off perpetually taking our own economic temperature, and forget ourselves in thinking about what we can do for the world!

THE CAUSE OF FREEDOM   March 22

How different today are the battlegrounds of freedom from those of the past! Just as old needs have changed, so old slogans no longer suffice.

The cause of freedom is no longer to be identified merely with the cause of the oppressed classes within the several nations. Rather does it involve, on the one hand, moral and cultural evils within our civilisation far more subtle and intractable (since prosperity can bring its own moral diseases), and, on the other hand, the relations of nations and races with one another.

And, when we have said this, we have said by implication two other far-reaching things. The one is that no sort of self-interest anywhere can serve the cause of freedom: if it did so in the past, it cannot do so now. The other is that the problem is not how this section or that section of humanity is to win freedom, as some of the past battles used to be, but how humanity itself, how man himself, can be free.

TRUE FREEDOM   March 23

Democratic institutions may indeed serve freedom, and may be the necessary condition of its advance, and yet to identify them exactly with freedom is too naïve. True freedom comes through men and institutions serving an end greater than themselves. Man is created in God's own image in order to fulfil himself in fellowship with his Creator. Having already a potential freedom, man's perfect freedom lies in his unifying all his powers in obedience to the will of his Creator, "whom to serve is perfect freedom".

Our various freedoms in politics and economics, for which liberators have striven in the past and will go on striving in the future, are not ends in themselves: they exist to serve man's freedom as the perfect discovery of himself in the use of all his powers in the service of God and his fellows.

DEEPER THAN TOLERANCE   March 24

Our western world is not yet free from the intolerance of race. Perhaps it is this which most of all calls us to go beyond tolerance and see the insufficiency of tolerance as a conception.

I need tolerance if I am to allow a man to have a different theology or different politics from my own. But if I am to allow a black man to live in my community, it is not a matter of allowing his opinions, but of allowing *him*; and while between my opinions and his opinions there can be an apathetic existence (which negatively is all that tolerance means), there cannot be merely that between one man and another man so long as the word *man* means what we believe it to mean.

The alternative to racialism is not tolerance; it is those deeper virtues in our Jewish–Christian tradition into which tolerance must merge if the thing and the word are to survive. (CEA)

WELCOME ONE ANOTHER   March 25
The separation of races in churches and in homes and in social life mars the character of Christian fellowship as the apostles understood it. Separation, whether in churches or in the homes of people, contradicts the doctrine, "Welcome one another as Christ welcomed you". In every country there is much to repent about.

If we exclude a man because he is of another race or colour, are we not excluding Christ himself? (CP)

SENSITIVITY AND KINDNESS   March 26
Alas, the trampling on human rights can happen more near at home, more easily and familiarly than in the great issues of the world. Every insensitive action towards another man or woman, every unkindness or thoughtlessness, is an act of violence to a fellow creature. It is treating a person like a thing, and to do this is to crucify Christ afresh.

FELLOW CITIZENS   March 27
We have, and we shall go on having in this country, citizens whose forebears have long lived in this country, and citizens whose forebears lived in one of the Commonwealth countries overseas. We are fellow-citizens whatever our place of origin, and whatever the colour of our skin.

But there is among us a good deal of race prejudice and colour prejudice, and the honour of our country demands that we should be rid of it. How shall we be rid of it? By tackling the practical problems which cause friction, and by knowing that the other man—whatsoever his race, whatever his colour—is a man created in God's own image, after God's likeness.

DO I CARE?   March 28

While we are pressing for peoples and governments to adjust their sights to a Christian vision and to the consequential Christian obligations, we find the voice of Christ speaking to our own consciences.

Am I ready for a simpler way of life? Am I ready for standards less well-to-do than we have had in the past? Do I myself care enough to be doing all I can in the service of the hungry? Do I care in a way that really costs me?

The picture comes before us of Jesus approaching the city of Jerusalem and weeping over it, for it did not know the things which belonged to its peace. We may picture Jesus today weeping over many cities, towns, villages, and countries: some with their poverty and hunger, some with their wealth, their power, and their complacency. The tears of Jesus unite our world and show us how bound in a bundle we are. Jesus would have us share in his grief, and if we are his followers we shall not wish it otherwise.

But those who share in the grief of Jesus are admitted to a share in his joy: his joy over one sinner who mends his ways, his joy over every cup of cold water given to a child who is in need, his joy over every act of true service to his heavenly Father and to mankind. We shall not ask, "Who is my neighbour?" My neighbour is Christ, and Christ is everywhere. (CP)

OBEDIENCE   March 29

We are servants, called upon to obey. Has not the idea of obedience as a Christian virtue rather slipped out of our contemporary religion?

We think much about the responses of faith, love, sonship, friendship in our relation to God or to our Lord. But obedience? We tend to think that it smacks of legalism, and not to dwell upon it.

But it has an ineradicable place in the New Testament. Jesus was "obedient unto death" (Phil. 2:8), and "he learned obedience through what he suffered" (Heb. 5:8).

The apostle is Christ's slave. It follows that, beside our responses with the motive of faith or love, there are also our responses with the motive of obeying God in doing this or that because we believe it to be his will. "If you love me you will keep my commandments" (John 14:15). (CPT)

MATTERS IMMEDIATELY AT HAND   March 30

When men do what is right in the particular circumstance, in the task at hand, in the details of what lies immediately before them, they may be building greater than they can ever know. It is not given to most men to see great visions, or to construct grand concepts. But it is given to every man and woman to make decisions about the matters immediately at hand, putting what is right before what is capricious, putting divine law before human wilfulness.

When that happens, God in his good providence gathers up our little actions of the moment, and uses them in his design down the ages. Did not Christ say that he who is faithful in little shall have great riches? The riches may be incalculable results in later times.

RELIGION AND COMPASSION ARE ONE   March 31

To turn to God is to turn to this man or that woman who is oppressed. To turn to Christ is to turn to this man or that woman in whom Christ suffers. Christ is the Christ who is found there. God is the God who is found in everyone who possesses his image. It is when our religion and our compassion are utterly one, it is when our sense of God and our care for humanity are utterly one, that things begin to happen. For our God is no one unless he is the God in every man, and our Christ is no one unless he is the Christ who suffers in and for humanity.

"What is man that thou art mindful of him?" Man is a being, every man is a being who has the weight and worth of eternity. And what is required of man? Let the prophet's words tell us: "He hath showed thee, O man, what is good. And what doth the Lord require of thee, but to do justly, and to love mercy, and to walk humbly with thy God."

APRIL

CHRISTIANITY'S INTRINSIC CHARACTER   April 1

The Easter faith, existential as it is, was and is related to history. Christians believe in the Resurrection partly because a series of facts are unaccountable without it.

Christianity entered history because of the Resurrection. Without it there would be no Christianity. And Christianity entered history as the religion of a crucifixion that was liberating and victorious.

This gives Christianity its intrinsic character: it is the gospel of life through death, of losing life so as to find it, of sacrificial love as possessing sovereign power. (GCW)

THE HISTORICAL JESUS   April 2

How may we approach the history of Jesus? Let us start with three facts which no reputable historian will want to deny. Jesus existed. Jesus died by crucifixion. Subsequently the phenomenon of Christianity came about.

Now history has to explain not only how Christianity came about after the crucifixion of Jesus, but also one remarkable characteristic of it from the start. It included a new valuation of suffering and death as being not the marks of defeat and disaster, but as things positive and creative. This is seen in the teachings, the liturgies, the ethics, the way of life, the practical behaviour of the Christians, and it is bound up with a conviction about the crucifixion of Jesus. This horrible event is not ignominy, defeat, disgrace; it is good news, a divine action which has brought salvation.

How did this conviction, integral as it was to the phenomenon of Christianity in history, come about? It is true that, according to the traditions within the Synoptic Gospels, Jesus gave to the disciples teaching about the significance of his death. But it is clear that up to the time of the Crucifixion they had not grasped his teaching or absorbed it. When Jesus died, the secret died with him.

Something happened, not only to cause the Church to recover and survive, but also to cause the astonishing assurance that the death of Jesus was good news. Something happened. The apostles said that what had happened was that Jesus made himself known to them as alive: they saw, heard, and received the impact of his person upon them as he gave them, not comforting illusions, but challenges to new actions and new understandings.

Either the apostles were deluded in their conviction that Jesus was with them again, and in that case their subsequent life and behaviour were rooted in delusion, or else it was really true that Jesus had risen. (CP)

FOUR PORTRAITS OF JESUS   April 3

While each Gospel draws upon the traditions about Jesus handed down in the Church as part of the general stock of Christian teaching, each of them is in itself a portrait with its distinctive features of portraiture.

St. Mark shows us the vividly human aspects of Jesus, who is none the less the divine Son who comes in power, and the intense emphasis upon the way of the Cross is in itself a part of the power of God at work.

St. Matthew shows us Jesus as the Royal Messiah, fulfilling the Old Testament, reigning in and legislating for the community of his disciples, and warning them of a final judgment both for them and for the world.

St. Luke shows us the ministry of Jesus's compassion, reaching out to meet every human need; and, while the story is very down to earth, it resounds again and again with the canticles of praise and songs of heaven.

St. John (and who dares to summarise his portrait in a sentence or two?) shows us that the Word who is made flesh in Jesus is also at work in all creation; that life and judgment are present in the here and now, and that the Passion is in itself victory and glory.

JESUS AND HIS CONTEMPORARIES   April 4

Though we cannot search the Gospels for biography or for diary memoirs, we are none the less able by scientific procedure to gain a picture of Jesus in relation to his contemporaries.

We ask what are the themes about Jesus which are well attested within a number of strands in the tradition, in sayings, in parables, in episodes. We ask that we may get a picture of Jesus in his various relationships with the scene around him. Thus, Jesus is one who searches for the outcasts in society and befriends them. Jesus is lonely, cut off from home and family as he pursues his mission. Jesus is vividly conscious of the presence, sovereignty, and graciousness of God in nature, and in the lives of men and women. Jesus shows that a new order is here breaking in, an order which fulfils the scriptures. Jesus predicts judgment upon the Jewish church. Jesus trains disciples to be the nucleus of a new Israel with whom a new covenant is made. Jesus accepts death as his vocation, and he sees beyond his death a divine victory depicted in a variety of images.

By this procedure we gain a picture of Jesus in relation to his contemporaries in Palestine. (CP)

Jesus demanded an obedience to the law far more radical than its official teachers understood: an obedience going to the roots of motive as well as to outward action, and involving positive acts of goodness as well as the negative avoidance of certain evils.

This meant that Jesus was bringing men and women into touch not just with the law, but with the God whose law it is, the God whose holiness requires total obedience to him, and whose compassion requires total compassion to others on any day of the week.

It was a message about God and God's sovereignty. It therefore cut at the heart of the idea that just to keep the law is the way to spiritual security. It is idle for the rich young ruler to say, "All this I have observed from my youth up". It is idle for the Pharisee in the parable to count upon fasting twice in the week and giving tithes of all he possessed, for righteousness is about God, and about humility.

The law cannot save. God, whose law it is, can save, and does. (CP)

"A GLUTTONOUS MAN ..."   April 6

Christianity broke upon the world with an impact at once intensely unworldly—indeed, other—worldly—and intensely down to earth. Jesus stood before his contemporaries as one who accepted the world and rejoiced in it, and as one who summoned men and women to a radical renunciation of it.

There is indeed a difference in tenor between the great plant parables and the appeal to the lilies and the birds in the Sermon on the Mount, and the sombre parables of the expectation of the lord as a thief in the night, and the terrifying predictions on the Mount of Olives.

Unlike John the Baptist with his asceticism of the desert, Jesus seemed as one who "came eating and drinking . . . a gluttonous man and a winebibber" (Matt. 11:19). He accepted the world as good, with his leisurely perception of flower, tree, bird, sheep, fox, sky, field, lake. He saw human actions as the scene of the divine presence. Sower, farmer, vintner, fisherman, labourer, shepherd, mason, housewife, and the soldier under authority—all are to him a parable of God's ordering of the world.

Domestic happiness, civil order and patriotism, and man just as he is with his imperfections, provide analogies for God himself. "If ye then, being evil, know how to give good gifts unto your children, how much more shall your heavenly Father. . . .?" (Luke 11:13). (SS)

A CRITERION OF THE REAL JESUS   April 7

In the first three Gospels Jesus is recorded as making stupendous claims for himself—chiefly by implication—and these claims lead on to the belief in his Messiahship and divine lordship. Yet Jesus is not making himself the centre of his message: he effaces himself in the service of God's kingdom, he is leading men and women beyond himself to God's kingdom and its righteousness, never to a kind of self-contained Jesus-cult.

Now to turn to St. John's Gospel. Here the claims made by Jesus are more explicit and more tremendous. "Before Abraham was, I am." "I and the Father are one." And these claims lead on to the great confession of Thomas after the Resurrection: "My Lord and my God".

But in this Gospel too, Jesus is pointing beyond himself, and it is to the Father that he leads us. He does not glorify himself; he glorifies the Father. "If I glorify myself, my glory is nothing." "I seek not my own glory, but the glory of him who sent me." And he leads the disciples on to a devotion to him which is not a Jesus-cult, but a worship of him only in union with the Father in the bond of the Spirit; only in the glory of the Triune God.

Jesus leads men beyond himself alone: this is always one of the criteria of the real Jesus.

TRANSFIGURED   April 8

"He brought them up into a high mountain, apart by themselves, and he was transfigured before them." It did not mean that he had left behind him the conflicts of the Galilean ministry which had gone before, or the conflicts of the *via crucis* which were to follow. That, perhaps, was St. Peter's error, longing to linger in the glory of the mountain scene and to leave all that was irksome down below. Rather was it that, when our Lord went up to be transfigured, he carried with him every conflict, every burden, to be transfigured with him.

And when *we* go apart to be with Jesus in glory, it is so that our frustrations, our pains and our cares may be carried into that super-natural context which makes all the difference to them. These frustrations are not forgotten; they are not abolished; they can still be painful. But they become transfigured in the presence of Jesus, our crucified and glorious Lord.

And when we have carried our frustrations up to our Lord in his glory, we find in the days which follow that he generously brings his glory down right into the middle of our frustrations. "My peace I give unto you." "These things I have said unto you that my joy may be in you, and that your joy may be full." "Be of good cheer, I have overcome the world." (CEA)

"THE MAN AGAINST RELIGION"   April 9

The Gospels show us that for Jesus there is no exclusion of his God and Father from any part of nature and humanity. God is found in the flowers and fields, in scenes of domestic life, in the reactions of little children, in the catastrophes of history.

But Jesus is seen, none the less, as religious man. It is his custom

70

to be in synagogue on the sabbath. He joins in the religious rites of the Jewish Church and nation. He prays often, apart, alone. And when he prays he draws upon the words of scripture and psalm.

Yet he also appears as the man against religion. He assails the religion of his contemporaries: a religion liable to be so encased with departmental professionalism that in the very middle of its zeal for the things of God it was forgetting mercy and judgment, and blinding men's eyes to the activity of God outside the religious camp.

Religion in its turn resents Christ and assails him, and it is by religion that he is done to death outside the gate of the city. In the desolation and darkness on Calvary he cries, "My God, my God, why hast thou forsaken me?" But in the desolation God is there, sharing and bearing the world's darkness. (SS)

SOMETHING HAPPENED   April 10

Without the Resurrection the Christian movement would have petered out in ignominy, and there would have been no Christianity. It is not too much to say that without the Resurrection the phenomenon of Christianity in the apostolic age and since is scientifically unaccountable. It is also true to say that without the Resurrection Christianity would not be itself, as the distinctiveness of Christianity is not its adherence to a teacher who lived long ago but its belief that "Jesus is Lord" for every generation through the centuries.

The Resurrection is something that "happened" a few days after the death of Jesus. The apostles became convinced that Jesus was alive, and that God had raised him to life. It is not historically scientific to say only that the apostles came to realise the divine meaning of the Crucifixion for them, or that the person of Jesus now became contagious to them. Something *happened* so as to vindicate for them the meaning of the Cross, and to make the person of Jesus

71

contagious to them. The evidence for a stupendous happening, which the New Testament writers mention, was the survival of the Church, the appearance of Jesus in a visible and audible impact on the apostles, and the discovery that the tomb was empty.

The several elements in this threefold evidence no doubt had different degrees of evidential weight for different people, and they have had such varying degrees ever since. As to significance: if it were the existential encounter of Jesus which alone mattered, then the empty tomb would have little or no significance. If, however, Jesus has a *cosmic* meaning with cosmic effects, then the empty tomb has great significance, akin to the significance of the Incarnation itself. (GCW)

TESTIMONY OF TRADITION   April 11

To read the Gospels in the "new" way which Form–Criticism has brought about is not to reduce their historical value for the life of Jesus, but to re-present that historical value in terms of an inter-pretative portrait which may none the less be a true portrait if the interpretation is a true one.

C. H. Dodd asked what were the features of the portrait of Jesus widely attested by a consensus of traditions about his actions, relationships, sayings and parables, and he gave this result:

1. Jesus's compassionate searching for the outcasts of society;
2. Jesus's loneliness, separated by his vocation from his home and family;
3. Jesus is in victorious conflict with supernatural powers of evil which assault many sufferers, his disciples, and himself;
4. Jesus by his presence in the world marks the line between the old order and the new;
5. Jesus is the fulfilment of the anticipations and hopes contained in the Old Testament;
6. Jesus brings divine judgment upon the nation.

I would not hesitate to add to the list, using the same scientific principles:

1. Jesus, whatever other titles he uses or rejects, speaks of a sonship of himself to the Father, intimate, and not identical with the general sonship of the disciples;
2. Jesus predicts his own death, not as a disaster, but as lying within the kingdom of God;
3. Jesus predicts beyond his death a divine vindication expressed in a variety of images;
4. Jesus summons his followers to die with him so as to share in the vindication. It will be a vindication of himself, of them, and perhaps of the human race ("Son of Man") with him.

The portrait is not the portrait of one whose biography can be constructed, though some of its episodes can with fair confidence be set in a sequence of before and after. It is an existentialist figure whom we are shown, one who challenges human existence with the divine judgment and the divine generosity. But it is also a real, visible, human figure, who challenges men not just as a kind of *incognito* within whom the deity is veiled, but as one who can be known in and for himself, and loved and imitated. (GCW)

THE RIGHTEOUS ONE   April 12

When Jesus disappeared from the world and vanished from the stage of history, people by and large thought, "Well, there he goes; there's one more impostor done to death, one more irrelevant interruption of life put away, perhaps even one more lunatic gone to his own place; anyhow, we are rid of him, and the world sees him no more." That was the average man's verdict on the strange story of Jesus.

The truth was that when Jesus disappeared from the world to die, he was the righteous one, and it was the great act of righteousness, love, and faithfulness, and the Father vindicated his righteousness in the Resurrection. The Holy Spirit brings people's hearts and minds round to perceive that the death of Jesus is the true righteousness: that's what righteousness is really like: suffering love.

CONCERNING JUDGMENT April 13

When Jesus died on the cross everyone thought that he was being judged. The Sanhedrin had voted him guilty, Pilate had condemned him to death, popular opinion jeered at him and condemned him, and indeed it must have seemed as though God himself had also condemned him by letting this happen. It seemed that the world had passed judgment on Jesus.

The truth was that Jesus dying on the cross was passing judgment on the Jews and the Roman Empire, on Caiaphas, on Pilate, and on every civilisation until the end of time. They are all judged by Calvary, and it is the work of the Holy Spirit to bring the world round to the conviction that Jesus crucified is the divine judgment upon them, the divine judgment upon all of us.

LETTERS April 14

The early Christians wrote letters. Especially the apostles, Paul, Peter, John, and others wrote letters to the churches which they had founded, reminding them of the great truths about the Gospel, advising them about questions of belief and conduct, and warning them against moral and spiritual dangers. Such were the *Epistles*. They were not written with a view to their becoming Holy Scripture or parts of a Bible. They were what we might call occasional letters.

But they came to have, and still have, immense authority for all Christians down the ages. Why? Because they gave first-hand witness to the truth and the power of Jesus Christ as it was known among the first generation of Christian believers. This witness is twofold. It tells of what Jesus *was* when he died and rose again—the sure basis of historic fact on which Christianity is founded. It tells also of what Jesus *is*, living and contemporary, the ever-present Lord of the Christians, with whom they enjoyed fellowship. When we read the Epistles we put ourselves with the first Christians under the power of Jesus who once died and now lives.

PERSONAL RESPONSE   April 15

There are parts of the Bible which can—more than some others—evoke a personal response, and turn our reading into wonder or worship: many of the psalms, some of the parables of Jesus, parts of St. John's Gospel (not least the discourses which begin "I am . . ."), and the Epistles of St. John. But each reader will find for himself what evokes his poetic imagination, his sense of wonder, his awareness of God.

Having so discovered, we do not rest content with what most appeals to us, for we must be led on to become learners from Christ in the scriptures. And we do not forget that the Christ who is the central theme of the Bible is the same Christ who feeds us in the sacrament of his Body and Blood, and is present in the world today, not least in those who suffer—to serve whom is to be serving Christ himself. The Christ of the Bible is ever near us, around us, and within us.

SPIRIT OF WORSHIP   April 16

The worship of God is itself the inner core of Christian spirituality: the heart, the mind, and the will, directed towards the glory of God as man's goal. Every time that a Christian lifts up his soul to God in desire towards him he is, however faintly, realising that fellowship with the Creator for which he was created, and he is, in a tiny and yet significant way, anticipating the goal of heaven.

Thus regarded, spirituality is no escape from the world. It is lived

75

out in all the complexities of our social life, in family, city, country, industry, culture, joy, sorrow, for it is the spirituality of a man, and a man is involved in all these things. It is inseparable from service, love, duty, the moulding of the common life. Yet in deep-down essence it is the spirit of worship.

Allow me to quote some words of a former Archbishop of Canterbury, William Temple. He said, "The proper relation between prayer and conduct is not that conduct is supremely important and prayer may help it, but that prayer is supremely important, and conduct tests it". (CEA)

It is sometimes said that conduct is supremely important, and worship helps it. No, worship is supremely important, and conduct tests it. That, I am sure, is the right order because God himself is man's goal and man's true end; it is for glorifying God that we are made. But because God himself is love and righteousness, we are not glorifying the God of truth unless our glorifying is being reflected all the while in the relationship of practical service in the human community in which we live. Such is spirituality in its true ideal. But the ideal has been distorted and wrecked by the fallenness of man and by human sin, bringing about its terrible distortion of the world order.

To deliver the human race from this distortion there came the Incarnation, Crucifixion, Resurrection, and Ascension of our Lord, and the gift of the Holy Spirit. It is in the redeemed community, in union with the divine-human Lord Jesus, and guided by the Holy Spirit, that the human race recovers its true function of worshipping and glorifying God.

But there is now this difference. For redeemed humanity, worship is not only the basic relation of creature to Creator, it is also the relation of the redeemed sinner towards the God who has redeemed and saved him through the blood of the Cross of Christ. 'O for a thousand tongues to sing my blest Redeemer's praise!" Thus the worship of Christians is not only the worship of creatures finding access to their Creator, but also the worship of miserable sinners thanking and praising God in Christ who has visited and redeemed his people.

GODWARD MOVEMENT   April 18

The Godward movement has many aspects. It includes the use of mind and imagination which we call meditation; it includes the counting of God's mercies which we call praise and thanksgiving, and the self-abasement which we call confession. But try to think of it more simply: it means putting yourself near God, with God, in a time of quietness every day. You put yourself with him just as you are, in the feebleness of your concentration, in your lack of warmth and desire, not trying to manufacture pious thoughts or phrases. You put yourself with God, empty perhaps, but hungry and thirsty for him; and if in sincerity you cannot say that you want God, you can perhaps tell him that you want to want him; and if you cannot say even that, perhaps you can say that you want to want to want him!

Thus you can be very near him in your naked sincerity, and *he* will do the rest, drawing out from you longings deeper than you knew were there, and pouring into you a trust and a love like that of the psalmist—whose words may soon come to your lips.

Forgive me for putting this so clumsily. I am trying to say that you find you are "with God", not by achieving certain devotional exercises in his presence, but by daring to be your own self as you reach towards him. (CPT)

CONTEMPLATION   April 19

Let us emphasise more strongly the contemplative element in prayer.

We used to think that discursive intellectual meditation was the kind of thing for all Christians to practise, but that the contemplation of God was something confined to mystics and saints and specialists—something that people should rather be warned off as being too dangerous or presumptuous.

I believe that the opposite is the case. I believe that discursive, intellectual meditation is a very, very difficult exercise, and you have to be rather clever to tackle it at all. I honestly have never been clever enough to do more than collapse at the first hurdle.

But the simple contemplation of God from the depths of the soul is something accessible to any Christian man, woman, or child. It is also, I believe, being better understood in the modern world, and—odd though it may seem—the contemplative element may be the instrument by which we touch and elicit the meaning of religion in our contemporaries.

NEAR TO HEAVEN   April 20

Now prayer is characteristic of piety, and it is plain enough that to be pious is not necessarily to be near to heaven.

As with works, so with piety. There can be good works done with zeal and energy, and yet there can be in them a self-conscious busy-ness or a possessiveness and patronage which leaves the doer in the bondage of self, and far indeed from heaven. There can be piety which dwells upon the man's own spiritual state and his self-conscious enjoyment of it, a piety concerned with its own exterior techniques or its own interior feelings, and the devout man can be far indeed from heaven. Philanthropy and piety alike may be nearer to hell than to heaven.

But wherever there are works in which God is present through the humility and charity of the doer, heaven is not far off. And wherever there is the prayer of a soul hungry for God, and ready in the middle of its own weakness and failure to be filled with God's own charity—the *vacare* (to be empty) being the gate to the *amare* (to love)—heaven is very near.

So not only among the conflicts of the world, but within the soul of the Christian as he prays, heaven and hell struggle together like the twins in the womb of Rebekah, and both are near to us at every moment. (CEA)

NOT A BOMBARDMENT   April 21

So many people think of prayer as a kind of bombardment. Do we want something? Let's decide what we want—some nice presents for my birthday, or peace in Ireland, or some other object, laudable or less laudable. Let's make up our minds what we want and set going a bombardment. If enough of us make these requests and—still more—if enough of us make these requests simultaneously, then God will yield to the bombardment and be good enough to concede the thing we are asking.

Isn't that rather what some popular ideas of prayer are like—organising a bombardment of requests?

But it is a wrong idea about God and praying, for two reasons. First it suggests that God is somewhere rather far away, and has to be reached by a kind of spiritual heavy artillery. And secondly it is wrong because it suggests that prayer is something we start with our own little ideas and requests. No, if God is Creator, Father, Friend, the Lover of Mankind, the real point about prayer is being in touch with him like the touch of human friendship; enjoying his presence, and being near to him so that a great deal passes from him to us and from us to him in a happy, joyful—though sometimes painful—intercourse.

If you think of yourself and a greatly loved friend, there may pass from you to him certain requests, and he may make certain requests to you. And you say "yes", or you say "no", but your intercourse with him is far deeper, more joyful, more comprehensive than that.

The words that you exchange are only a small part of what is exchanged simply by presence and happiness and the mutual impact of person on person.

April 22

You may say, "Oh, but I don't feel God to be near like that. I just don't get the sort of religious feeling that some people get—the prayers and hymns and all that. To me it's just blank."

Well, leave out any idea of feeling pious; no one wants you to feel pious. Leave out the word God if you like. It is you, and the realities you know. Deep down in you there is a sense perhaps of tremendous obligation, things which are a "must" for you because they are right. So, too, in the lives of others there are things which you admire tremendously, with reverence and awe. Then from time to time there is the horrid sense of guilt: something I am meant to be and I have wilfully failed to be. Then, in some of the crises of the world you remember a conviction in you that something is right and is therefore meant to prevail. And with all these experiences there is often a sense of wonder, wonder at something, someone, intimate with you in the depths of your being, and yet beyond, far beyond. It is all this which, for me, adds up to the word God, especially when I consider the person of Jesus as gathering up the whole. But perhaps for you, though it all means so much to you, and the heart of the matter is in you, there is a kind of emptiness, a blank, a hunger.

Now, it is just this emptiness, blank, hunger which can find any of us nearer to God than a spate of consciously religious feelings. No one is nearer to God than the man who has a hunger, a want— however tiny and inarticulate. And that is where prayer can begin, the prayer of simply being oneself in utter sincerity. One can pray like this: "O my God, I want you: help me to want you more." "O my God, I love you so little; help me to love you as you love me." "O my God, I scarcely believe in you; increase my tiny faith." "O my God, I do not really feel sorry for my sin; but I want to. Give me a true sorrow for it." (MP)

ACCEPT HUMILIATIONS   April 23

Be ready to accept humiliations. They can hurt terribly, but they help you to be humble. There can be trivial humiliations. Accept them. There can be bigger humiliations: some cherished plan misfires, or some injustice is done to you, or some slight and affront, or some sorrow, or some trouble caused by a mistake of your own. Accept them.

All these can be so many chances to be a little nearer to our humble and crucified Lord. There is nothing to fear if you are near to our Lord, and in his hands. (CPT)

LAUGH ABOUT THINGS   April 24

Use your sense of humour. Laugh about things. Laugh at the absurdities of life. Laugh about yourself and about your own absurdity.

We are all of us infinitesimally small and ludicrous creatures within God's universe. You have to be serious, but never be solemn, because if you are solemn about anything there is risk of you becoming solemn about yourself. (CPT)

CRITICISE YOURSELF   April 25

Take care about confession of your sins. As time passes, the habit of being critical about people and things grows more than each of us may realise. So be sure to criticise yourself in God's presence: that is your self-examination. And put yourself under divine criticism: that is your confession. Then God's forgiveness renews your freedom to be humble.

If you use sacramental confession, do not slip out of using it. If you do not use sacramental confession, ask yourself if it would not be a good thing that you should. (CPT)

THANK GOD   April 26

Thank God, carefully and wonderingly, for your continuing privileges, and for every experience of his goodness.

Thankfulness is a soil in which pride does not easily grow. (CPT)

CONTEMPLATION IS FOR ALL   April 27

Mystic experience is given to some. But contemplation is for all Christians. Allow me a word about that prayer which is indeed for all of us.

The prayer of Jesus our high priest is classically described in the sentence "he ever lives to make intercession for us". Now, the Greek word which is here, and elsewhere, translated "intercede" does not mean to speak or to plead or to make requests or petitions: it means to *meet* someone, to *be with* someone in relation to or on behalf of others. Jesus is with the Father, for us.

And our own prayer means essentially our being with God, putting ourselves in his presence, being hungry and thirsty for him, wanting him, letting heart and mind and will move towards him, with the needs of our world on our heart. It is a rhythmic movement of our personality into the eternity and peace of God, and no less into the turmoil of the world for whose sake (as for our own) we are seeking God.

If that is the heart of prayer, then the contemplative part of it will be large. And a Church which starves itself and its members in the contemplative life deserves whatever spiritual leanness it may experience. (CPT)

It is in the measure in which the contemplative spirit is in the Church that the reality of God will be grasped within the Church's multiple activities. *"Contemplare et contemplata aliis tradere"* (to contemplate and pass on to others what you have seen) was a maxim of St. Dominic. But the practice of this maxim demands a will for leisure and passivity in the midst of ceaseless activity—a will *vacare considerationi* (to give space for contemplation).

I recall the words of Fénelon in a letter to a French duke of the time. "I want to help you find how to lead a very full and yet leisurely life." That is a prime requisite for Christian spirituality in the modern world. (CEA)

CONTEMPLATION AND ACTION   April 29

How are contemplation and action to be blended together?

Both belong to the life of the Christian community in the world. Because the Christian community has the duality of this-worldliness and other-worldliness, there are inevitably within the Christian family those who are called specifically to contemplative lives, and those who are called more specifically to lives of energetic service to their fellows. But both belong to the totality of Christianity in the world, and the life of the Christian community is a kind of rhythm of coming and going, like Christ leading three chosen apostles to the Mount of Transfiguration, and thence descending to the hard way of the Cross, the Father being present at every step in the coming, the going, and the returning.

And if there is this rhythm in the total life of the Christian community, it is a rhythm which must needs be produced within the life of every Christian. While Christendom has contained those who have told us in great depth about the mystical and contemplative life, and those who are leaders in the realm of Christian action and service, so there have also been Christians who have been preeminent in the borderline of these two vocations, showing how the two are held together. (SS)

"Jesus is Lord." That is the faith which we proclaim on the lovely festival of the Ascension—Lord in his sovereignty, Lord in his presence.

It was indeed for the advantage of the disciples, and for our advantage, that he went away. And throughout the life of a Christian this law of Christ's parting, this law of gain through loss, will often recur. We learn something of Christ's truth, we enjoy his presence, and then sometimes he may seem to leave us, and we lose touch with him—for he would not have us rest complacent where we are, but press on—perhaps through loss and desolation—to new perceptions of his purpose for us.

So again and again Christians find that Jesus leaves them, and the divine cloud envelops him, and we await the new tasks which he has for us.

MAY

THE CHURCH'S TASK   May 1

The Church is pledged to influence society and to criticise society.

In this task its deepest influence should always be upon persons in their character as persons. Christ himself lived and died and rose again in a world full of social abuses, including the appalling abuse of slavery. But Christ's chief method was not to attack institutions, but to transform people. And there can be no substitute for the impact of Christianity upon people at their deepest level, always remembering that a person never lives in a vacuum; he is always a bundle of social relationships, both private and public, and these relationships all need to be Christianised.

So the Church's mission to change personal lives cannot be separated from its critique of wrong attitudes in society.

IN THE HEART OF THE SECULAR WORLD   May 2

The Christian Church with its members has the difficult but fascinating task of living in the heart of the secular world, coming alongside all the good which is there, and at the same time lovingly upholding a critique of the secular world in the light of the supernatural.

Inevitably this critique will be more lived than spoken. Christian supernaturalism will carry with it as a very part of itself the will to "muck in" with the secular, while living the life that is "hid with Christ in God". In the apartness of his own contemplation of God, the Christian will be aware of the true end of both himself and those whom he is serving.

But just as Christ took upon himself the form of a servant, and the divine glory was not diminished but rather revealed, so it is with the Christian Church. "The action of the Church," writes Daniel Jenkins, "is sheer worldliness however much it may be dressed up in religious garb, unless it is covered with the holiness of Christ, and the holiness of Christ is always found on earth in the form of a servant." (SS)

HOW ARE CHRISTIANS DIFFERENT? May 3

Suppose that we Christians were more truly fulfilling our difficult mission towards secular society, what might a good, decent secularist or humanist begin to say about us? What sort of idea of us would we like him to have if the Church of God and its members was more what it ought to be towards secular society?

I might overhear someone saying this: "These Christians behave rather differently from what we used to think. They are interested in the things that interest us. They care about them. They share them with us. They are good at them. They do not preach at us and tell us that we are wrong in our assumptions. But they begin to make us feel we *are* wrong in our assumptions by being the sort of people they are. They share our work with us. They are always alongside us. They really do know. They really do care. But they bring to it something different, something different which makes us think."

And what is that "something different" that Christians are meant to bring? I believe there are three things, each of them very much down to earth, but each of them springing directly from the other-worldly experience of Christianity. The first is a deep reverence for persons as destined for eternity with God. The second is a kind of heavenly serenity which is able to draw the sting of suffering. And the third is the humility of a man or woman who has known authentically the presence of God.

IN THE CONTEXT OF ALL MANKIND   May 4

Christianity teaches us that when we have troubles of our own we see them aright when we see them as part of the wider, vaster troubles of mankind as a whole, and when we remember that there are parts of the world where sufferings are so great that our own can scarcely be called suffering at all.

We in this country are not starving; we are not very poor; we have a high standard of living; we have many luxuries. So try to picture those who have a few mouthfuls for their families to eat every day: a few mouthfuls. Indeed, our own troubles and conflicts might be nearer solution if we had not been so long obsessed with taking our economic temperature over and over again, and so getting our values wildly wrong.

If we at this moment have our troubles, what a chance it is to see them as a little bit of the world's troubles; what a chance to see, to care about, to *feel* the desperate plight of others in the world. Again and again I find the apostles in the New Testament writing, bidding the Christians of their time to think of the greater conflicts, the greater hardships of their brethren in other lands. We are—we really are—members one of another. (CP)

A NEW TASK OF LIBERATION   May 5

The problem of plenty and poverty (and the bitter contrast between them) has largely moved from being a matter of classes within a nation, such as ours, to being a matter of nation and nation. In parts of the world a comparatively high standard of living is shared by all classes, and in other parts of the world there are whole populations dangerously near the famine line.

Here lies a new task of liberation: for the wealthier nations to come to the service of impoverished nations. It is here that love of freedom has to prove itself, by exporting and creating freedom in places where it is thwarted or in peril.

We speak of the "free nations", of the "free world", but the reality of those descriptions turns upon their power to export and create the freedom they enjoy—whether in the relief of the impoverished, or in the bringing of ordered freedom to races hitherto governed by the "free nations".

Indeed, to create and export freedom is the only way to defend it.

To a Labour Party Conference, 1960

SERVANT AND HELPER OF OTHER COUNTRIES   May 6

The Christian will want his country to be the servant and helper of other countries. He will be concerned to see his country doing all it can for the help of the impoverished peoples, especially where hunger is acute. He will want to emphasise that if his country enters a group of nations, say a European group, formed for their mutual benefit, there must be the utmost concern at the same time for the help of the underdeveloped and poor countries.

And the Christian, knowing that human fulfilment is bound up with obedience to divine love, will watch carefully the concept of freedom and the claims made for it. The "free world" does not properly mean just a group of nations which have escaped the Communist yoke. The freedom with which Christians are concerned is achieved not just by democratic institutions, but by democratic institutions disciplined by the highest ideals.

And freedom cannot be defended by building a rampart round it.

It survives by its power to give itself creatively to nations which lack it, a giving which will include both things material and things spiritual. It is thus that the West must look towards Africa and Asia, and give of its best to them while there is yet time. (CEA)

"SUPREMACY" UNDER JUDGMENT   May 7

There is the place of South Africa in our consciousness.

I agree with those who say that, in a world filled with many varieties of evil and injustice, it is wrong for us to become obsessed with any one particular country. Yet South Africa is bound to loom large in our consciousness, because its regime claims to be a bastion of Christian civilisation and to represent that civilisation on the African continent, and also because South Africa is the most tragic outcrop of a phenomenon we all share, the phenomenon of white supremacy in history. We are part of an era of history in which the white man has been supreme, and even now we can tacitly be sharing in the assumptions of that superiority. Southern Africa is the part of the world where that supremacy is challenged, and where the challenge is being resisted with violence by government.

We must realise that any attitude on our part towards either violent or non-violent policies is going to be very costly for us if we try to be Christian. If we say to Africans, "Do not act rashly. A violent revolution is likely only to bring terrible suffering to yourselves," we are saying in effect, "Go on accepting your present suffering". And we can say that to people only if we somehow are ready to suffer with them.

If we say, "Why don't you fight?", then we may be advocating something we may not ourselves be aloof from, something which could be a widespread war with hazards about its outcome. In either case, our opinions will be Christian and ethical only if we are ready to identify ourselves, and somehow to share in the pains of it all. (CP)

We may urge that the best chance for social change in Southern Africa lies not through war or the ostracism of any regimes, but through contact with all the influences that may come through social and trade relationships. If so, we must remember that there are forms of contact which help the situation and forms of contact which do not.

It does not help when white immigrants go and fill the jobs which should be filled by skilled Africans. It does not help to make investments unless such investment is designed—as is sometimes possible with difficulty—to help African advancement. It does not even help, as some of the Churches in Southern Africa have found, to subsidise education, unless it is for an educational syllabus which aids advancement and not down-grading.

I believe that contact rather than ostracism can achieve something, but it needs to be contact in the right way and with the right care. Otherwise contact may only serve the bolstering up of injustice. (CP)

GOD IS ABSENT   May 9
When men and nations turn away from God's laws and prefer the courses dictated by pride and selfishness to the courses dictated by conscience, calamitous results follow. God is not absent from the contemporary scene; he is present, present in judgment through the catastrophes which follow human wilfulness.

And nowhere is the divine judgment *as* the working out of human folly put more trenchantly than in the words of the Psalmist: "So he gave them their heart's desire, and sent leanness withal into their souls". (CPT)

CHRISTIAN OPINION   May 10
There is the need to create opinion through Christians together showing that something is absolutely contrary to the Christian way

of life. But all the time it is supremely important for the Church not to be a set of people with negative things to say, but a set of people who point to Jesus Christ himself.

Show us Jesus and he will be the inspiration, the challenge, and the goal. Show us God himself in his greatness and goodness, for there, and there alone, is the true perspective for man's life.

ARROWS OF DESIRE   May 11

Anywhere, everywhere, God is to be found. In your daily encounters with people, God is there. You can recollect him, you can be with him, you can share your doings with him; you can shoot arrows of desire from your heart to his. (CPT)

THE TRUE RADICAL   May 12

Remember that some of us older men were once the progressives, or even the radicals, and now we are outmoded. If you are one of today's progressives or radicals, you will be outmoded soon.

The true *radical* is not the man who suspends himself from the branches on either the left or the right, but the man who in his thinking and action goes to the *root* of the tree.

In many ways the younger and the older learn from one another. Maintain your integrity, your power of criticism: be yourself. And at the same time let humility, forbearance, and a love of people, both young and old, help you to enjoy and to strengthen the fellowship across the decades. (CPT)

THE FAMILY IS PART OF GOD'S SCHEME   May 13

We who are Christians believe that the family is part of God's scheme of things

When men and women take part in the procreation of children they have the wonderful privilege of sharing in God's creation of

91

human life, and they are called to do this in God's way. And God's way means that procreation takes place not anyhow, but by a man and woman who are joined together in a lifelong union, a union in which they give themselves to one another until death parts them. That is the atmosphere of love and stability into which, in God's design, children are born.

And having been born into a family, they are loved, cared for, and protected, and they grow up in the freedom and discipline of mutual love and care for one another. So when children go out to take their part in the world, their role in their own family is not left behind, but lasts as a permanent part of their lives.

The happiest families are not introverted and wrapped up in their own circle, but outgoing as part of the wider community. (CP)

EXCITING AND DANGEROUS   May 14
Family life and marriage are not a fortress to be defended so much as an exciting and dangerous adventure.

To the Mothers' Union, 1970

BOND OF UNION   May 15
Sex in marriage is the means whereby children are procreated and also the bond of union between two personalities. Both those things are desirable in the fulfilment of marriage. In the perfect marriage both are meant to be there, and it is wrong to avoid either. They are meant, but they aren't so totally linked that sexual relations are unlawful apart from the procreation of children.

When you ask "What's right?", there are relativities. The use of sex in respect-full human relations is certainly better than the use of sex in selfish, irresponsible enjoyment. But Christianity is concerned with the best, and—I think rightly—defines its ethics by asking, "What is it that God wills?" And that is using sex within marriage.

Reply to a question at the London School of Economics, 1970

What are the facts and principles upon which monogamy rests?

Male and female—the difference of gender belongs to many parts of nature as well as humanity. It links humanity with nature, and also serves humanity's divine goal, which reaches far beyond nature. The delicate division of gifts and qualities leaves man eager for woman, and woman eager for man. Eros, or love, is the desire of the one for the other, as the one feels incomplete without the other; it is a desire to possess and be possessed. Venus is the pleasurable act in which union is expressed; it serves Eros, and Eros craves for it.

But Eros and Venus together do not exhaust the meaning of man and woman in their togetherness. Man and woman are selves, they are persons; they bring to one another a wealth of thoughts, actions, interests, concerns, and these are to become the stuff of the unity between them, without individuality disappearing. What monogamy does is not only unite Eros and Venus to one another, but unite them both within the whole realm of unities in which man and woman can be joined.

Thus it is that these are linked with *Philia* (friendship), the whole range of comradeship in life, together with all that this involves. And as God is the giver and God is the goal, there comes also within the relationship of man and woman the *Agape* (the word which is usually translated as "love" in the New Testament, especially in 1 Cor:13) which is the divine self-giving kind of love without which the rest may go astray.

Such is monogamy. Its emergence in history, its interior depth, and its stable continuance require the sacrifice of a great restraint. (CEA)

Conscience in man is a God-given thing. The operations of conscience can be perverted, and its findings can be distorted by wrong assumptions. Yet it is always a phenomenon to be reverenced because it is God-given, and the Christian duty of educating consciences in the light of Christian truth goes with this reverence for them.

Not seldom has it happened that Christians have found themselves corrected by the consciences of pagans, and the will to admit this need not weaken the claims made for Christian revelation. (SS)

CULTIVATED "RELIGION"   May 18

"Religion" can mean a sort of specialised area of life wherein things to do with Christian belief and worship are enclosed as a sort of departmental *corpus*. Forms of worship, books, sacred buildings, sacred arts; professional functionaries from choirboy to archbishop; the vocabulary, the technical terms and modes of thought; the moods, attitudes and feelings of devout people—all these together form the professional culture of Christianity.

Taken singly, each item on the list may be good and worthy as well as inevitable. Together they form a pious *corpus*, and we know how big can be the distance between being a Christian and being a person about whom it is said "he is interested in religion", or, "he is so interested in religion that he is not interested in anything else".

It goes with a form of idolatry which I think largely lies behind the "death of God" talk, of which we have heard much in the last decade or so; the idolatry of supposing that God is immensely interested in religion and religious activities, and feelings about what goes on inside churches and temples, forgetting God's intense and immense interest in everything that happens in the world: that God cares as much about what is going on in the market place, the village green and the workshop, the factory and the mine, as he does about what is going on in the sanctuary, or in the religious activities of religious people.

How true it is that the great Christian realities of faith, love,

94

repentance, and prayer, can have built around them a world of
pious culture such as can all too easily smother them! (BR)

THE DANGER OF IDOLATRY   May 19
Had it occurred to you as a Christian that idolatry is always our
real danger?

Not the idolatry of worshipping wood and stone—"the heathen
in his blindness bows down to wood and stone". You aren't very
likely, I suspect, to be doing that. No, we Christians are prone to
a far more terrible idolatry of nominally worshipping the true God
who is the Father of Jesus, but in fact turning him into an idol
through the inadequacy of the concepts in our hearts and minds as
we worship him. The crudest way of doing that, to which we are all
prone, is to think of God when we pray, and unconsciously to read
our own pettiness and selfishness into the picture.

If our thought of God and our prayer to God is mixed up with
narrow, perverted, selfish ideas, limited visions of him and his
purpose caused by a kind of lethargic selfishness and insensitivity
to humanity on our part, then we may be using all the right formu-
lae—possibly having the correct images in our minds—but really
doing what the Israelites were doing when Moses came down from
the mountain and found they had made a golden calf, and were
worshipping the golden calf instead of the true God.

THE THREE ELEMENTS OF SPIRITUALITY   May 20
The Benedictine way of life, though it was a way of life for
monastic communities, gives a pattern applicable to all Christian
life. First of all there is the principle that work and worship go
together—"*orare est laborare, laborare est orare*" ("to pray is to
work, to work is to pray")—the complementary character of the
worship of God and the service of man. But in worship there are
three great unchanging factors. One is the Eucharist; the second is

the Scriptural Divine Office; the third is personal prayer. That is the Benedictine triangle.

The Eucharist is the great act in which the Church commemorates Calvary, finds Calvary present and in its midst, and in union with Christ crucified offers its life and the life of the world to the Father. The whole people of God participates in this act of thanksgiving, offering, and communion. That is the centre of Christian spirituality. Indeed, the Eucharist is really the Lord's Prayer—the Paternoster—filled out in a great act.

The second element, the Divine Office, is the element of worship drawn from the synagogue, and it is scriptural through and through. The Divine Office means commemorating God the Creator and the Redeemer in psalms and canticles, meditating upon the divine revelation in readings from the Old and New Testaments, and responding to this in acts of prayer and intercession.

This scriptural Divine Office is an essential undying element in Christian worship, using the scriptures to commemorate God, using them as a means through which God feeds the souls of Christian people, and responding to them in prayer and praise.

Of course, that element comes into the Eucharist itself, but the supremacy of scripture which meant as much to St. Benedict as it must have meant to Cranmer, is emphasised in the *opus dei*— "seven times a day will I praise thee because of thy righteous judgments".

The third element is personal prayer, and in this—because no two Christian souls are alike—every Christian soul must be itself in praising and praying; always within the common life of the community, but each man and woman making his or her own prayer from the depths of their souls. While it is important that every Christian's prayer should be within the common life, it is also important that it should be his very own prayer and her very own prayer: the self coming to fulfilment in that marvellous individuality which God created.

96

There is the Benedictine triangle, and that is the classical shape of Christian spirituality in the West.

In the later Christian West the triangle got distorted and corrupted in a lot of ways.

The Eucharist—the Mass—got rather lop-sided because of the increasing non-participation of the people in communion, and through the rather distorted ideas of sacrifice, particularly in relation to purgatory. Then, because the Latin language was used, the Divine Office became a kind of non-starter as far as the laity were concerned. The scriptures were still read, and private prayer still went on, but the shape was distorted. Some of the glories of medieval spirituality are found in personal prayer, mystical prayer, spiritual reading—and sometimes of a glorious sort—but they were unrelated to that pattern of common life which had been the Benedictine way.

Then came the Reformation. All sorts of things happened in different parts of the Reformation scene: the Anglican Reformation claimed to recover the Benedictine triangle and present it in a new way—not in relation to the monastic life because monasticism was, alas, abolished—but in relation to the common life of the Christian Church.

The spirituality presented by Cranmer in the Prayer Book was, I believe, a recovery in a new cultural context of what had been the Benedictine shape. For what do we have? We have the Eucharist, and the book of Common Prayer assumes that it is celebrated every Sunday and every saint's day and holy day. Then there is the Divine Office, and this in Cranmer's Book of Common Prayer is tremendously emphasised. Morning and Evening Prayer are substantial presentations of the Divine Office. In Morning Prayer the psalms and the first lesson give us the acts of God under the Old Testament, and then the *Te Deum* comes as a great commemoration of the Incarnation—"Thou art the King of glory, O Christ", and then the second lesson tells more about the divine revelation in Christ and the apostles; then the *Benedictus* or *Jubilate* gathers it up into the Creed. It is a great presentation of scriptural Christianity to which people respond in praise and prayer.

So, too, Evening Prayer has the same pattern. There are the psalms and the lessons of the Old Covenant; then comes the Incarnation commemorated in the song of Mary herself, "*Magnificat anima mea Dominum*"—"My soul doth magnify the Lord"—and then the teachings of the new revelation are gathered up in the *Nunc Dimittis*—"for mine eyes have seen thy salvation". And the people, feeding their souls as well as their minds on the scriptures, respond in prayer and praise.

Then there is the third element, private prayer, which has always been emphasised in the Anglican tradition, and many of the prayers and collects in the Prayer Book presuppose the fact of private prayer, and ask for grace to do it better. Yet, in the Anglican tradition, there has always been a certain kind of reserve, perhaps a lack of enthusiasm, a lack of ardent devotion. That is why Roman Catholics and Methodists often find something a little cold in the Anglican devotional tradition. It is due to the kind of Englishman's reserve and shyness that translates itself into his religion.

STAYING WHERE YOU ARE CALLED TO BE   May 22

To St. Benedict nature was good, and worship meant not a flight from God's good works, but the praise of God for them, and the offering of them back to him.

His community was devoted to the praise of God thus conceived, and it was not a collection of individuals seeking perfection, but a family. The self was to be forgotten in the brotherhood of a common life, and with the worship of God there went the daily work wherein God claimed the common life as his own.

Characteristic, too, of the Benedictines was the concept of *stabilitas loci* (stability of place). Instead of the restlessness of the desert monks roaming from place to place to escape the world and themselves, the Benedictines emphasised staying where you are called to be and consecrating life *there* to God's honour and presence.

Benedictinism is an ascetic life, in poverty and celibacy, and with a particular emphasis on obedience; but it is an asceticism reaching near to humanism. It is significant not just as a species of monasticism, but as an epitome of principles of Christian life applicable to different forms of Christian calling. (SS)

FELLOW-WORKER WITH GOD   May 23

We ought, while continuing to believe in man's creatureliness, to emphasise also his vocation to grow through sonship into being a fellow-worker with God, and thus to share as a son in the Father's creative process.

Too often our piety can fall short of that, and can indeed remain childish. But let man grow into his role as a mature son and fellow-creator and he will still be liable to sin, and will at times need to be prostrate before the holy and forgiving God. The greatness of God is such that the bravest and strongest will find themselves little in his presence.

It is one thing to be childish, with a religion which never grows up. It is another thing to be childlike, with a religion which matures into a manly independence, and yet discovers an ever-deepening dependence upon God as our origin and our goal. (CP)

DARKNESS AND THE LIGHT   May 24

The Bible uses the word "darkness" for human evils of many kinds.

It is darkness when people care for prosperity and material things and ignore the things of the spirit.

It is darkness when people who are rich and prosperous do not care about those who are poor and hungry.

It is darkness when nations and races are full of fear and suspicion, hatred and even war.

It is darkness when moral standards, like the unity of the human family, are being eroded.

It is darkness when drug-taking wrecks people's lives.

In the middle of this situation Jesus Christ says, "I am the light of the world". Jesus calls his disciples to follow him and, going with him, to see.

It is characteristic of Christians that, following Christ, they can see and help others to see.

From a sermon in Singapore

BEYOND THE SKY AND EVERYWHERE   May 25

For the biblical writers and for much Christian thought in post-biblical times, heaven or the other world was a place beyond the sky. Thither Christ had gone up at his Ascension, and there the saints reigned with him in dazzling light. It was another world related to this world astronomically, which really meant that it was part of this world.

Yet within this language of locality, just because it was language about God, there was present something which strained it and turned it into the symbol of realities which transcended locality altogether: the supremacy of Christ everywhere, and the union of Christians with God through him. The right hand of God meant no local activity, but a symbol of God's sovereign power. The Ascension of Christ meant a presence unrestricted: if he is here, he is there; if he is there, he is everywhere. God being "above" meant a relation no less describable as "within". The spatial conception of the "other world" lingered, but the heart of Christian belief knew from the beginning that it was only using symbols for the God–Christ–mankind relationship beyond locality.

So the "otherness" of the other world is not that of a structure standing over against this world. It is the otherness of man's life with God, invisible, present already, and leading to a destiny after death. Just as the approach to the belief in immortality is through belief in God ("God is the strength of my life and my portion for ever"), so man knows of and approaches the "other world" through fellowship with God, a fellowship which is the other world's essential content.

That other world—heaven—has God's own glory, reflected in his perfected children, as its very essence: *quem nosse vivere est* (whom to know is to live). Hence no language suffices to describe it, since to describe it is to describe God whose reflection it is.

THE HOLY SPIRIT   May 26

We as Christians know how the birth and life and death and resurrection of the Lord Jesus, God and man, led on to the great outpouring of the Holy Spirit at Pentecost.

In the New Testament the Holy Spirit is primarily the Spirit given by Jesus to the members of the Church to carry on—through the redeemed Christian community—that cleansing, that sanctifying, that making-lives-holy, that restoring lives to the proper divine pattern and making them ultimately fit for heaven again in spite of everything.

That is what we Christians are primarily thinking of when we say, "I believe in the Holy Spirit, the Holy Spirit who sanctifies me and all the elect people of God".

THE COMFORTER   May 27

In our modern Christianity we have rather shrunk from using the phrase "the Comforter" for the Holy Spirit because we think it sounds soft and cosy, a sort of divine molly-coddling. But we have to remember that when Jesus said the Holy Spirit is the Comforter there was a particular background to his words, the concept of divine comfort in the Old Testament which Jesus draws upon and applies in his own new way. "The Lord will comfort Sion"; "Comfort ye, comfort ye my people, saith your God." And the prophets and the psalmists look forward to the divine comfort coming to Israel.

What did that divine comfort mean? It was the coming of peace, the coming of prosperity, the crops growing, plenty in the land, food to eat, good harvests, no more famine, no more drought, and so on; all that can be desired, real and lovely comfort for the people of Israel. But it also meant God reigning in Israel, the banishing of injustice, of wrong, of evil, of sin, and the establishment of a true divine order in which unrighteousness, injustice, cruelty, quarrelling, greed, envy, and uncharity were banished from the land. Thus the divine comfort meant nothing less than the whole blessing of Messianic salvation coming to the people. It meant the divine peace, but linked inseparably with the divine righteousness.

So when Jesus prophesied that the Holy Spirit would be the Comforter it meant that the Holy Spirit will bring us peace indeed, peace and joy, but the peace and joy from above, the peace and joy of Jesus, the peace and joy which comes when our wills obey God's will, when sins are forgiven, when there is that true inner harmony with God, in whose will is our peace.

Thus the meaning of the comfort of the Holy Spirit is seen when our Lord says, "Peace I give unto you; not as the world I give unto you". Christ's sort of peace, and Christ's sort of joy comes into human lives. (SS)

WIND AND FIRE   May 28

The imagery about the Holy Spirit is largely impersonal—wind and fire, fire that blazes, wind that blows—and I think we should remember this impersonal imagery and not be ashamed of it. We need it because it is the imagery of the dynamic and the unexpected, of a mighty power doing for us far beyond what we would imagine to be possible. Fire that blazes, gale that blows. But we find that among this impersonal imagery the New Testament writers begin quite naturally and spontaneously to start speaking of the Holy Spirit as a person: a He, rather than an It.

It is because the Holy Spirit is so linked with the person of Jesus that the Holy Spirit is personal too, and we find this astonishing unveiling of the truth that somehow the Holy Spirit is a person just as Jesus is a person, and just as the Father is a person. The Spirit is personal: God within us responding to the personal God outside us. Thus, "Grieve not the Holy Spirit".

The Spirit wills, the Spirit purposes, the Spirit advises, the Spirit counsels, and above all the Spirit prays. When the early Christians prayed, they came to realise that it wasn't just God beyond them (and they praying out of the strength of their own wits and perseverance); no, somehow it was God within them enabling them to respond in their prayers. Our great passage about this is in Romans, chapter 8, where the Spirit prays in us who are Christians with groanings that cannot be uttered; and specially the Holy Spirit prays in us the very prayer of Jesus: "Abba, Father". That was the heart of Jesus's own prayer, the prayer of sonship, "Abba, Father".

The Holy Spirit described impersonally as wind and fire is no less personal, reproducing in us the very prayer of Jesus, and so enabling us to have the greatest gift that Jesus wants us to have, namely *sonship*. Because you are sons, God has sent the Spirit of his son into your hearts crying "Abba, Father".

FLAMES OF FIRE   May 29
    Think of yourself on a cold, dark night. You slip into a room. No lights are on. It seems dark and cold. But presently just a little light, just a little warmth reaches you. You move closer. A fire is burning.

You begin to see. In the brightness of the fire you notice in the room shapes, forms, outlines. If there is someone else in the room you see his face, reflecting the fire. Thus the Holy Spirit enables you to see, and to see like a Christian—perceiving things as they really are in the eyes or mind of Jesus; perceiving people as they really are with the light of Jesus upon them; perceiving meanings and purposes instead of shapeless confusion; perceiving what a Christian ought to be doing.

Remember the words in the *Veni Creator*:

> Enable with perpetual light
> The dullness of our blinded sight.

Remember too the words in the Whit Sunday Collect where we pray that the Holy Spirit may give us "right judgment in all things". The Holy Spirit keeps the light of Jesus glowing in us: that is how we may see as Christians should see.

The fire, as you approach it, gives you warmth. Warm itself, it makes you warm. So the warmth of the love of God within you can warm your heart to love him in response. This is not a matter of sentiment only. The very love of God can penetrate you and warm your faculties to love him. So we say:

> Thy blessed unction from above
> Is comfort, light, and fire of love,

and an old Christian writer speaks of *incendium amoris* (love's kindling).

We remember St. John's words, "We love because he first loved us". This does not merely mean that, having heard about God's love, we are excited to love him in return: it means that the very love of God creates in us a love which is both our own and also his within us. Such is the meaning for all time of the "tongues like flames of fire" which sat upon the apostles' heads at Pentecost. (CP)

Light, warmth—and burning, too. The Holy Spirit will burn us. If we are to have vision, and if we are to have warmth of love, we must be exposed to the pains of burning. All that is fearful, un-loving, selfish, hard, must be burnt out of our existence, burnt to destruction, burnt to ashes.

While we think we have some Christian sight and knowledge, and while we think we have some warmth of love, there are within us unpenetrated barriers of selfishness and prejudice which resist the grace of God and thwart the light and warmth of the Spirit. The Spirit will burn his way through to the core of our being in the ever painful process of disclosure, of penitence, and of divine for-giveness. Only by such burning can our heart be fully exposed to the warmth, and our mind be fully exposed to the light. There is no seeing and no warming without that burning. It is thus that we realise the saying of Jesus Christ found in one of the apocryphal documents: "He that is near me is near the fire". (CP)

Extraordinary things happened at Pentecost. They started speak-ing with tongues as the Spirit gave them utterance.

That is sometimes understood as meaning that they had a mira-culous gift of languages, that those who only knew Hebrew or Aramaic suddenly knew how to speak Greek or Latin or some other language. I think this is unlikely. It is more likely that speaking with tongues at Pentecost meant what speaking with tongues meant in other passages in the New Testament: an ecstatic kind of utterance. In the power of the Holy Spirit they expressed themselves in words and songs of praise that weren't any particular language at all, but were just a kind of outburst of sounds, partly speech and partly music, giving expression to their common intense joy in the Holy Spirit. And we find, subsequently, that where people were converted to Christianity, this speaking with tongues used to occur.

But we also find that later on, in the Church of Corinth, when there were Christians who spoke with tongues, St. Paul gave them some advice on the subject. He clearly acknowledged that speaking with tongues was one of the gifts of the Holy Spirit, and an authentic sign that the Spirit is there. He told them that he could also speak with tongues and do it as well as they could. He also told them that speaking with tongues was a special gift, the value of which depended upon there also being people present with the gift of understanding or interpreting the tongues. And he told them this: that while the tongues are a gift, there is a greater gift than any, and that is love. Love—charity, self-forgetfulness in the common service of the community—is the greatest gift of all.

JUNE

THE TRINITY   June 1

The God to whom we pray is the Triune God, the blessed
Trinity, the Three in One and One in Three, not because theologians have invented a kind of mathematical puzzle to entertain us,
but because God so loved us that he gave himself in Jesus; we
worship Jesus without idolatry because he is true God; we worship
the indwelling Spirit because he is God no less, and in that worship
we are worshipping a God who is one.

The difficulty, if it be a difficulty, about that trinitarian doctrine
is not the difficulty of a mathematical puzzle, but simply the difficulty of comprehending a love that goes so deep. The Father, Son,
and the Holy Spirit are one in the oneness of love beyond all our
understanding, though that love has touched us and we have tasted
of it in the coming of Jesus, and in the operations of the Holy
Spirit in us and for us through the centuries.

AWFUL REALITY   June 2

We hear so much glib talk about God and glib discussion of God.
Talk, talk, talk. Books, books, books—about God and God's nature.

107

It is the awful reality of God that can be so missing from the talk about him, and can often be missing in our own talk about him as preachers and priests. Would that this dimension of divine reality were more present in our worship, and our preaching, and our dealings with people, so that people would more readily say, "Surely the Lord is in this place".

STRENGTH, CARE, AND TENDERNESS   June 3

On the west front of the cathedral of Chartres in France there is one of the most beautiful sculptures in the whole world. It is a sculpture called the "Creation of Adam", and in it the hands of God are depicted resting upon Adam's head as he moulds the first man into existence. And in the hands is a wonderful strength and care and tenderness almost unbelievable in their execution by the sculptor's craft.

Well, the love of God means that that strength and care and tenderness of the Creator rests upon every single one of us. God cares for you all that much, and this infinity of his care and strength rests upon you, and you are there at all only because of the great love of God for you. And you survive at all only because of his great love for you and the purpose of your existence—an existence for all eternity to which this visible life is only a little prelude. And the purpose of your existence is that God cares for you so much that he wants you to have fellowship with him forever.

That is what the love of God means, and let the realisation of it really come home to your imagination when you hear or use those words, and you will find it makes a difference. You will find yourself humbled to the dust; you will find yourself full of gratitude; and you will find that the whole scale of priorities and concerns in your life may be turned upside down because the first thing—the love of God and your response to it—will indeed come first.

It is very hard for us in the twentieth century to enter into the mental processes or the motives of those who designed and built our great medieval cathedrals. A love for God most certainly was there. So too was a devotion to the Church as an institution as powerful over men's minds and actions as any monarch or state could be. Perhaps also there was the concern for insurance about the hazards of the life to come, where the sombre stretches of purgatory preceded the bliss of heaven. Perhaps also the motive of jealous local patriotism had its part, as "our" church must be no less large and no less beautiful than those in other places.

So with mingled motives, but with the love for God certainly powerful among them, they built this minster.* And with mingled motives it has been loved through the centuries, by some with definite and ardent Christian conviction, and by some with a less defined sense of history and beauty, and by many with thoughts no more and no less than that it is *our* Minster, and we love it. Yet there must be few at any period to whom this church has not at times spoken of something beyond the material boundaries of material life, something which says, "Lift up your hearts". (CP)

"EXPERIMENTAL CHRISTIANITY"   June 5

Not seldom have people been led to suppose that the Church means the buildings, and that their upkeep is one of the primary Christian functions. Indeed, Christianity can itself appear to be identified with a particular sort of western European culture, with its chancels and naves and organs and pews and hassocks. Hence it is not surprising that—in reaction—forms of Christian fellowship are today springing up apart from the historic institutional Churches, with Christians meeting in houses to worship and pray together, to study the Bible together, to break the bread together, feeling after the mood and atmosphere of the first Christians.

* York Minster.

"Experimental Christianity", as it is sometimes called in contrast to institutional Christianity, may prove to be a growing phenomenon in our time. Indeed, it may be that the ecumenical task of the future will be less the holding together of the various older traditions—Catholic, Anglican, Protestant—than the holding together of the old institutional Churches on the one hand and the experimental types of Christianity on the other.

What is certain is that exciting days for Christianity lie ahead. (CP)

MEETING PLACE OF BELIEVERS   June 6

We think of the Christians of the first century. They meet in one another's houses to pray together, to celebrate the Eucharist, to listen to letters from an apostle, to practise fellowship in every way. Or sometimes they meet in the open air, near to some river or stream in which converts are baptised. *They* are God's house, and they know no other. The great cathedrals are not yet.

We can think, too, of how today there are Christians in countries of great poverty who have the simplest churches built of wood or mud, and they love them dearly and walk many miles to worship in them. Or we can think of countries today where Christians are severely persecuted, and once again it is the homes of the people that are the meeting-places of the believers.

In all these ways Christians have shown—and Christians show still—that it is the people, not the buildings, that make the Church of God. There are places in this country—not least in new areas of population—where this is most strikingly so. (CP)

LIVING STONES   June 7

Every Christian church was built because there exists this other Church of which St. Peter tells. Listen to his words: "Come to Jesus, to that living stone . . . like living stones be yourselves built up a spiritual house". That is what the word *church* meant to the Christians of the first century: not stone or brick or wood, but the Christian people themselves.

Jesus, rejected by men and done to death on Calvary, but precious in God's sight and now raised from the dead, is the cornerstone, and when men and women are converted and baptised they are united to him, and there grows, stone by stone, a spiritual house: Christ's home, Christ's temple, through whom Christ is now made known to the world. (CP)

MAN'S OFFERING   June 8

We need not apologise or regret that when Christianity moved into the world's civilisations and cultures in order to try to bring Christ's Spirit into them, there followed the baptism of painting and music and letters and architecture into the service and praise of God: man offering to God the greatest beauty he has to offer.

Man's works, as well as man, are claimed by God, and brought to him. Hence the story of Christian art, sculpture, and architecture through the centuries: never with the Godward motive absent, but always with that risk of mingled motives that belongs to man's fallible nature. (CP)

CHRIST'S BODY   June 9

The Christian Church has had many titles, and one of its most striking descriptions is "the Body of Christ". What does that mean? Well, there is a terrible literalness about it. It means that, just as Jesus, when he lived in Galilee and Jerusalem, had a body of flesh and bones and blood through which he lived and worked and showed himself to the world, so now after the Resurrection, Jesus—though out of sight—still has a body through which he lives and works, and carries out his purpose in the world. And the body is now composed of baptised Christian men, women, and children.

"THEY ALL BELONG TOGETHER"   June 10

Complex is our ecumenical scene today.

The historical Churches are more than ever involved with one another, more than ever discovering a common Christian consciousness, yet hampered by the weight of their institutional past, and looking forward for renewal to deliver them into a better service of Christ, and a breakthrough towards union. Yet renewal includes the challenges of experimental Christianity, and not a few younger Christians would dismiss both history and form, and be impatient of any interest in church structures, whether they be separate or uniting.

It is a scene with much muddle and confusion. But it is a scene in which the Spirit of Christ, the Spirit of love and power, and indeed of truth, is mightily present. We may be bewildered, but we need not be afraid. (CP)

VARIETY AND DIVISIONS   June 11

The divisions among Christians came about through many historical circumstances. When a Church becomes stale and badly in need of a fresh wind, the attempts to reform it can take a breakaway form through sheer impatience and eagerness to get on with it. So splits take place. Or Christians can follow some leader with a name, and idolise him; and that means a split.

Has there been some gain in variety not diversity? Yes, there has. But has there also been damage through our divisions? Of course there has. In particular it has sometimes made Christianity seem ludicrous when its adherents worship separately under different labels in different buildings in the same town or village.

But today the weariness with our divisions has been growing, and the strongest forces in Christianity are truly those which make for unity.

GROWING INTO UNITY June 12

Once for all Christ gave to the church the unity and the truth which are his. Yet through the centuries the church is sent to grow into the perfect apprehension of the truth, and to realise perfectly a unity which is to be wrought out amid the diversity of nations and cultures, and of temperaments and religions and intellectual experiences.

The ecumenical task is never rightly to be described as if it were like the reconstruction of a toy once made in its completeness and subsequently broken. Had there been no quarrels in the Church of Corinth, no schisms in the church, no great schisms between East and West, there would still be the growth through years of spiritual and intellectual struggle into the fullness of the unity which Christ once gave. (FCC)

BECOMING ONCE MORE THE CHURCH OF THE
RESURRECTION June 13

When St. Paul, writing to the Ephesians, elaborated the metaphor of the Body of Christ, it was a metaphor of growth from childhood through adolescence to maturity. Grace is given to each of us, and to each Church among us, "according to the measure of Christ's gift". The gifts differ, but they are all for the equipment of the people of Christ, for the work of his ministry, for the building up of the Body of Christ.

The full unity of faith, the full knowledge of the Son of God, the full mature manhood, the full stature of the One Church, is far in the future—perhaps never to be attained, according to the fullness of Christ, by the Church militant here on earth. Bodily growth comes as each part, each Church, does its own distinctive work faithfully, and so helps to build up the whole body with love.

We have all caught something of that vision afresh, in every Church. We are alive and seeking one another in a living and growing faith and love. We, the Churches, are becoming once more the Church of the Resurrection.

EACH TO ANSWER FOR HIMSELF   June 14

There can be no sheltering for us behind one another, nor even behind the Church.

The searching light of our Lord's loving and relentless eyes compels each one of us to answer for himself for the deeds he has done, is doing, and will do, in the flesh. It is the saving reality of our faith that each must bear his own burden.

In the time of each man's testing, the judgment is not of the Church but of the churchman; not of Christianity, but of the Christian; not of theology, but of each man's own knowledge of God.

"Lord, is it I?" It is as we confess that he restores us to life and bids us love one another, and feed his sheep.

EARTHEN VESSELS   June 15

Our faith should be free from any false triumphalism in the institutions which represent it. Churches do not have a glory of their own, or a power of their own; they are not called to dominate. They are the earthen vessels conveying faithfully but often imperfectly the power of Jesus Christ, whose Lordship is in the form of a servant.

"We preach not ourselves, but Christ Jesus as Lord."

STATUS IS IRRELEVANT   June 16

Status is the most irrelevant thing in the Church of God, and the lust for status is one of the most loathsome ways in which the spirit of the world can infect the life of the Church. The only status for any Christian—the only status for any priest—is that of the unspeakable privilege of nearness to Jesus.

"If a man serve me, let him follow me, and where I am there shall my servant be." That is the only status that we are allowed to think about. "If a man serve me, where I am there shall my servant be." "If a man serve me, him will my Father honour."

SENSITIVE CONCERN FOR TRUTH   June 17

We need in our Church a sensitive concern for truth, and an integrity of mind.

Looking back to the last century, we can see the blunders made when the historic Christian faith met the new sciences of evolutionary biology and historical criticism. It took some years of trial and error to discover that these new sciences did not annul, but rather enhanced, the wonder of the divine creation of the world and of man and of the truth of God's revelation through the Bible. The moral is that God teaches us not only through sacred theology, but also through many kinds of knowledge which we call secular, and through the happenings of history. We must therefore be more ready for the sort of processes of theology and faith which happened in the last century to be repeated in new ways, and we need to ask how we may learn today from sciences and movements outside the Christian Church, and so be learning of Christ who is still the image, the son, the wisdom, the word, of God.

But we fail terribly as teachers of the Gospel of God if we cause our hearers to be so obsessed with contemporary questions and conflicts of opinion as to miss the witness and authority of the saints all through the centuries who have known God in Christ. There can be not only a tyranny of the past, but also a tyranny of the contemporary, and it is from this that our Christian creed frees us into the freedom of the communion of Saints in every age, and in heaven. (BR)

It is possible for Christians to bear shocks and not to find them wholly destructive.

It has been characteristic of our Anglican portion of the Holy Catholic Church to learn from episodes of human thought without becoming in bondage to them. It was possible to learn from the Darwinian revolution in the last century a greater understanding of the divine process of Creation without becoming dominated by a dogma of automatic progress. It was possible earlier in this century to learn from the rigours of New Testament criticism without submitting to the liberal theory of Harnack or the scepticism of Bultmann. So, too, some of us have faced the message of a Kierkgaard or a Karl Barth, and through the deep darkness have learned more fully of the greatness of God and the nothingness of man, and have emerged not disciples of Barth's system, but people who see their old faith in new depth.

So today it is for us to be ready to find God, not within the cosiness of our own piety, but within the agony of the world, and the meeting of person with person every day. But wherever we find him he is still the God who created us in his own image, and sent his Son to be our Saviour, and to bring us to the vision of God in heaven. (ION)

LEARNING FROM EACH OTHER   June 19

Today the different Christian traditions are learning more and more from one another. We Anglicans are learning a great deal from Roman Catholics, from the Eastern Orthodox tradition, and from the different Protestant traditions.

And we observe with pleasure some signs that they are now saying things that have something a bit Anglican about them—in the old-fashioned sense. Here are some instances which I hope are not presumptuous.

We Anglicans notice in the Protestant Churches the emergence of a far more strongly liturgical tradition, which makes this linking of theology, preaching and liturgy a far from Anglican monopoly. Theology in terms of liturgy is something that the Protestant Churches have been rediscovering.

Then, looking at the Church of Rome, we see things happening which we dare to say have something just a little bit Anglican about them. There is the strong emphasis in the decrees of the Second Vatican Council upon the Holy Scriptures: the treatment of the relation of Scripture and tradition in rather a new way, and the treatment of the Church and collegiality, setting the Pope in the context of collegiality—that is something a good deal nearer to the Anglican way. Then there is the drawing out of the participation in the liturgy of the whole *plebs Christiana*—the turning of the liturgy into the vernacular, which was something the Anglicans did centuries ago. Not least we observe within Vatican II and some contemporary Roman Catholic trends the emergence of the idea of a hierarchy of dogmas, the recognition that in such a hierarchy the dogma of the Fatherhood of God and the Incarnation of Jesus Christ—true man and true God—is, as a dogma, centrally more important than, let us say, the dogma of the Immaculate Conception of the Blessed Mother, which we would say, if it is true, is deductive rather than central.

Now, as a result of this flowing together of traditions the Anglican claim to be a sort of bridge Church in Christendom has been somewhat undermined. We used to claim that Roman Catholics and Orthodox and Protestants were so far apart from one another that if they wanted to meet they must first have an invitation to go out to tea with the Anglicans and meet one another on Anglican ground or on a kind of Anglican bridge, as if we Anglicans were to say— perhaps a little too cock-surely—"We are the people whose mission is to bring you all together". In a sense that was true, and in a sense it goes on being true, because Anglicanism is a tradition with strange affinities with Rome and with Orthodoxy and with the Protestants and with radical Christianity. But the role can be less and less self-consciously pursued because, in this age of ecumenical renewal, all Christians are learning from one another, and all are being renewed in spiritual and intellectual movements which affect all of us.

What then is the Anglican role in the contemporary situation? I think the Anglican role is to go on being ourselves, humbly asking God to use us if we are faithful to what we have received. And if we go on being faithful, God will use us, and other Christians may be grateful for what God does through us—so long as we are not boastful, and do not make too many exaggerated claims. But I believe that the Anglican spirit in theology is still the spirit of a reconciling role. We are here as Anglicans to try to be reconcilers between old traditional trends, and new and more revolutionary trends in theology.

RECONCILING ROLE   June 20

There is a great danger that Christendom might split into two camps, a split cutting across all Churches—a split between traditionalists who go on in the same way with folded hands, and revolutionary, experimental Christians who part company with traditional shapes and formulations.

I believe there is something that Anglicans can do here, not as an Anglican Church so much as by fearlessly applying the Anglican spirit and temper: not to be afraid of new experiments which are very new indeed; not to be afraid of listening to God speaking in the secular world around us, but all the time upholding two things as guiding beacons. One is the fact that we are creatures made by a Creator in his own image, and that worship of a Creator by his creatures is something absolutely fundamental in the meaning of man and of Christianity. The creatures worship the Creator: keep to that and Christianity will not lose its bearings. The other thing is "Woe is me for I am undone for I am a man of unclean lips because mine eyes have seen the King, the Lord of Hosts". It is the sense of sin, the need for forgiveness, the centrality of the Cross in personal religion and as a key to our understanding of God and the world. Keep to that also, and we shall not lose our way.

It is the Anglican role to keep those things alive, and we do it by emphasising strongly that place of prayer and worship and liturgy which we still conserve, even in new and more revolutionary forms. Conserve it. Always keep our theology linked with the way of prayer, because it is in the way of prayer that we are kept to the creature's worship of the Creator, and to the sinner's gratitude to the Saviour.

NOURISHMENT AND EXCITEMENT   June 21

Another reconciling role for the Anglican spirit is in the use of scripture, the interpretation of the scriptures, and the preaching of the scriptural faith.

Here we have the same controversies and tensions: the contrast between a rigid near-fundamentalist literalism on one hand, and on the other a kind of Bultmann (demythologising) way of using Holy Scripture.

It is for Anglicans to be faithful to their threefold cord of scripture, tradition and reason: not to be afraid of letting reason find newer and newer understandings of what the scriptures mean and say, but still using the scripture in the context of tradition. That does not mean that we use the ancient Fathers as the authoritative guide, but that it is as a worshipping and praying community that we read and use the scriptures.

Let the scriptures speak for the nourishment of our souls as well as for the exciting of our intellects. Be faithful to that, and we shall be of some reconciling help in the many conflicts about the understanding and use of the scriptures which are so excitingly, hopefully, and dangerously happening in our own day.

There is the widespread idea that man is competent by his own powers to organise his own progress and happiness. It is a strange idea, inasmuch as the world is deeply divided and unable to rid itself of terrible weapons of destruction. Yet the idea is there because man does not sit back and ask himself the question "*Quo tendimus?*" (in what direction are we going?) so much as press on, absorbed in the use of his powers and the fascination of them. The mind which enjoys its own creations in discovery, in technology, in the organisation of human welfare can become too busy and absorbed to question man's own competence. Hence in the middle of man's mature intellectuality there is the pride and the insensitivity to the Spirit of God which creates what we call "modern secularism".

Then there is the tendency for modern man to live in a whirl with his mind overcrowded. There are so many more things nowadays to think about, and so many impressions entering the mind in rapid succession, while there are still only sixty minutes in each hour, and only twenty-four hours in each day. Hence the mind of man tends to lose its freedom, and to be ruled by the flux of impressions and sensations. I sometimes think that in the circumstances of the modern world an important part of our Christian asceticism needs to be the discipline of the mind to secure its freedom, even more than the discipline of the body.

As a result of the loss of touch with God, there is a deep frustration and fear, often subconscious, and always divisive in its effects upon man's soul. (CEA)

THE SECULAR WORLD June 23

The changes of the last few decades have produced the phenomena known as the "secular world" and the "secular mind". The word "secular" properly means no more than "of the age", and every generation in history is inevitably "of the age". But one of the marks of the new phase in our culture is the lack both of affection for past tradition and of concern for a world beyond this. There is a mentality so insulated within its own secular frontiers as not to be concerned either with the past or with eternity. It is these phenomena which give to the word "secular" its new shades of meaning.

Illustrations of the new "secularity" come easily to mind. There is the widespread rejection of morality presented in terms of authority. There is the lack of interest in the ideas of the previous generation, and a dimming of a sense of history. There is the belief in the omnicompetence of the technological sciences to explain man and serve his needs. There is the rejection of those otherworldly undertones which affected the outlook of earlier civilisations. And, of course, religious beliefs, practices, and institutions are dismissed as devoid of relevance or meaning.

Such is the atmosphere which surrounds western Christianity today. We must of course avoid exaggeration, for secularism by no means occupies the whole scene. The lines are often blurred, and the frontiers are not rigid. Both in the United States and in Britain much from the older traditions still survives and shows creative power. In America there is still considerable practice of religion, as is seen in the habits of church-going, and in a degree of public interest in religious questions which is reminiscent of middle-class Victorian England. In England only a very few people would call themselves atheists, and while a minority have Christian convictions which they could express and defend in a meaningful way, such pattern of ethical tradition as exists is a pattern derived from an earlier Christendom.

But the ethos of secularism is strong and contagious, and the efforts of Christian evangelism often meet what can seem to be an almost impenetrable mass of secular-mindedness. (GCW)

GOD MAY BE HIDING   June 24

We often use the antitheses—the Church and the world; the believers and non-believers; the Christians and the heathen, and so on—and they are very real antitheses.

121

Just now we are very conscious of the gulf between the Christian community striving to follow Christ, deeply believing in God the Creator, and trying to put their lives at the disposal of the Holy Spirit, and of the world in general which—as we say—couldn't care less—a world in which there is division, nationalism, racialism, imperialism, and the new phenomenon of modern secularism; which is a sort of way of life or mode of thinking about life which seems to leave no room for those things which we believe about God and about religion.

Thus we are tempted sometimes to think that we are in a circle of light, and around us is the great darkness of the world. But don't let us forget that God created the world: that the world is God's just as the Church is God's, and that if we are to carry the Christian Gospel to the world we shall never do it if we think of it as carrying the Christian gospel into a sort of dark, empty desert.

No, when we carry the Christian Gospel into the world we carry it into a world where God is already there waiting for us. We go to the world to find God there, just as we go to the Holy Communion to find God there. God is really there at work, sometimes in strange unexpected ways. Sometimes it is for us Christians to be startled by the presence of God where we hardly expected it, just as Moses of old was startled by the bush catching fire and telling him that God was there.

UNCOMPROMISING PROCLAMATION   June 25

Secularism is a very stubborn and difficult thing. By secularism I mean the mentality of a society, or part of a society, which rejects God, which rejects any concern for religion, and which frankly finds our talk about God and religion unintelligible.

So what do we do? There are certain things for us to preach and proclaim quite fearlessly, and not for one moment would I relax the fearless uncompromising proclamation of our supernatural God. But when we proclaim our Gospel to the secularist world, let us

remember that in the secularist world God may be hiding somewhere after all, and if we find him there we can be learning things
as well as teaching things.

WORLDLY MAN   June 26

The "worldly" man is not necessarily the depraved man. He is
the man who is misled into treating the world's goods as absorbing
ends in themselves, and so misses the awareness of meaning and
purpose beyond them.

The "unworldly" man is not necessarily the devout man, or the
man with conscious concern for God or for heaven. He is the man
who is not absorbed in the world's goods or dominated by them, for
there is in him an imagination or a simplicity or a humility or a
care for persons which hints at something beyond. His unworldliness is properly seen not in any neglect of the world, but in the
nature of his care for it. (SS)

READY FOR THE UNEXPECTED   June 27

Sometimes it happens that, when you make friends with a person
who calls himself a secularist and pooh-poohs God and religion as
irrelevant, if you really get to know him and win his trust, and
talk in mutual respect, and let him talk, you may discover that deep
down in him there are things that he reverences and cares about:
things he feels are a real obligation for his ideal of life and the
ideal he would set before his children. He is reaching out after
something that really is of ultimate meaning and concern, though
he would never use our sort of language in putting it to himself.
And it is sometimes possible to have a conversation—I know,
because I have had many—in which it is possible for the Christian
to say, "Yes I see; that's how you put it. I do see what a tremendous lot it means to you; but you know it is not so very different
from what we Christians mean by sin, or grace, or God".

Don't let us doubt that God is present in human lives, working perhaps at inaudible levels in the experience of men and women. We must never carry the Christian Gospel to people without reverencing the divine image in them, and we must be ready for the unexpected and unlikely to happen in terms of the presence of God in them.

CARE OF MAN FOR MAN   June 28

Above all there is the *care of man for man* within the secular world. It is apparent on all sides, and there is probably no state or social system within which it is not to be found.

Now the values at stake in man's care for man can differ between a Christian and a purely secular outlook, and they commonly differ deeply. The Christian's care for man has regard to the eternal worth of a man's destiny in fellowship with God, and this may cause the Christian and the pagan to make different judgments about what is good for man.

And yet, wherever there is in the secular world a genuine concern of man for man, *there* is something basically God-given, and if it is inadequate or misleading the Christian will correct it and deepen it only when he has first reverenced it for what it is. (SS)

"BE STILL AND KNOW THAT I AM GOD"   June 29

There is, for us whose hearts God has touched, the supreme task of bringing home to the people God himself in his majesty, his compassion, his claim upon mankind, his astounding gift of his very self in Jesus, the Word made flesh.

We cannot fulfil the task for this country unless we are striving to fulfil it towards the whole of the world. It therefore demands the service of men and women who will go anywhere in the world in Christ's obedience, who will witness to Christ's love in the insistence that races, black and white, are brothers together of equal worth.

Here at home our mission means for the Church a constant involvement in the community. We shall strive to penetrate the world of industry, of science, of art and literature, of sight and sound, and in this penetration we must approach as learners as well as teachers. We need to be learning not only many new techniques, but also what God is saying to us through the new and exciting circumstances of our time.

Yet, because it is God to whom we witness, we need no less a constant detachment, a will to go apart and wait upon God in quiet, in silence, lest by our very busy-ness we should rob ourselves and rob others of the realisation of God's presence.

"Be *still*, and know that I am God." Would that everyone whose heart God has once touched would guard times of quietness in our noisy, bustling life, to let God touch the heart again. Is there a more urgent need than this for every layman, every priest, or bishop or archbishop in our Church? (CEA)

GOD CAN FILL OUR EMPTINESS   June 30

We don't find God by trying to be more religious than we are or can be. No, we are near God by being true to ourselves in all our experiences, and then God can begin to find us and to fill our emptiness. And some of the old phrases of religion can be near to what is in the heart.

"O Lord, thou hast searched me out and known me. Whither shall I go then from thy presence?"—God finding me.

"Make me a clean heart, O God"—God making me fit to be near him.

"O God, thou art my God, early will I seek thee"—wanting God more than I ever thought I did.

"Praise the Lord, O my soul, and all that is within me, praise his holy name"—being grateful for all this, and wanting to say how grateful I am. (MP)

JULY

RELIGION IN SCHOOLS   July 1

I would keep religious instruction in schools for two reasons. One
is that although our country no longer has a population adhering
to Christian convictions, such ethical pattern as we have is derived
from Christianity. Therefore we need an understanding of Christianity for an understanding of ourselves: who we are, and where
we are going.

The second reason is this: religion is a phenomenon, some understanding of which is absolutely necessary for man's understanding
of himself. And if religion is to be understood, then it must be
through understanding some *one* religion from within; for attempt-
ing to present "religion" in an amalgamated form always results in
presenting the virtues of none of them, and therefore doesn't really
succeed in presenting the meaning of any religion at all.

EDUCATION THAT MISSES OUT   July 2

How far is this or that kind of education giving a chance for the
appreciation of religion—the attitude of religion—to form itself and
grow in a child's mind? It is not simply a question of whether this

or that is being taught; it is a question of what modes of thought, what processes of knowing and appreciation are being elicited, and what ideas about life and its purpose are being stimulated.

There is the tragic fact that a good deal of education gives little or no place to the processes of thought, knowledge, and imagination whereby religion can be appreciated. The mind is stuffed with facts, but the use of the imagination in wonder and in the sense of mystery is not evoked.

The mind is trained to approach knowledge exclusively along one or two tracks, the tracks of science or technology: and to a mind so trained the language of religion is a foreign language conveying little or nothing.

We must face the fact that there are thousands of young people so educated that our problem is not just that they don't know the Christian faith, but that their minds are so formed that it is the hardest thing for the Christian faith to be intelligible to them.

The attitude of religion is in large part the sense of wonder: wonder at man, wonder at the marvel of his capacities and his frailties; wonder at man as he learns about the universe around him, and uses and misuses his knowledge. Hence we pass from wonder about man to wonder about the world with its astonishing range of content from atom to saint, and then to wonder about the Maker, both of man and of the world.

EVERY PART OF TEACHING   July 3

We who are concerned with religion, in our approach to teachers of every kind and every subject, should not let them think that religion in education is confined to hours and syllabuses with the label "RK" or "RE". Quite unselfconsciously every part of teaching can be religious, and can be preparing the soil for religion.

Elicit from your pupils wonder, imagination, the sense of the mysterious about the world and man, the realisation that there are different ways of knowledge—and the way is being prepared for the realisation of God. Religion has at its root the power to make you laugh at yourself, and to wonder at your own existence. "I am fearfully and wonderfully made."

THE WHOLE PUPIL   July 4

I now say something about our teaching of religion, and it applies wherever we do it: state school, church school, college, where you will.

Let it appeal to *all* the pupils' faculties. It includes facts for the mind to absorb and the memory to retain; it includes pictorial imagery for the imagination to see—not only in the pictures of events in which God revealed himself, but also in the poetic imagery which fills the language of religion through and through. It includes a person to be known and loved as a person, and that is why again and again Christ as he was in the Gospel story must needs be linked with Christ as he is as our contemporary Lord. It includes, as we have seen, mystery evoking the sense of awe and wonder. It includes moral demand speaking to conscience—but the more this is realised naturally and inherently, without moralising, the better. It includes the constant evoking of thought, questioning inquiry.

What great demands on the teacher! They are tremendous. And the teacher alone cannot bear them. That is why they have to be borne collectively by teacher and school—and by home and church as well, all together. But the teacher *can* have an eye to all these needs—and must.

NO PAT ANSWERS   July 5

Avoid like the plague any idea that, while in other subjects we ask questions and have queries, in religion the answers are all "pat", and questions are not wanted. That is fatal. Good religious teaching awakens the mind from question to question: about the meaning of it, about the corollaries of it for thought, life, and duty.

The child's religion must grow and grow and grow, and so must the religion of all of us. It must grow in intellectual questioning, whatever the risks and worries and doubts, and it must grow at the same time in the deepening sense of worship and dependence.

Our terrible casualties are due to religion not growing: perhaps the worship being ardent and at the same time the mind being stifled and static, or perhaps the mind being clever and critical, but the soul starved in the knowledge of God through prayer and sacrament.

Yes, but can the religion of the child grow except as a part of the growing life of the family of the Church, young and old together?

CHRIST FOR THE YOUNG   July 6

In every part of the world young people are revolting against tradition. They will not believe things or do things just because they are told to. They want to explore and to discover for themselves, and it is necessary that they should be encouraged to explore and discover as much in the realm of religion as in other spheres.

The young must be presented with a Christianity which is not a set of negative prohibitions, but rather a positive adventure. Young people will see that Christianity is not an old and tired tradition, but a new and exciting adventure. It is an adventure of service to Christ and to humanity, and when it is presented like that it appeals to the generous impulses of the young.

It is in that way that the young people will be drawn to the Christian faith, and the joy and excitement of the Christian life.

THE ROOT OF ALL ILLS   July 7

While Christian people strive to heal the world's ills by their service and charity, it is for them also to point to the ill which is at the root of all ills—the estrangement of the world from God—and to witness to the reality of God himself.

They do so by the depth of their communion with him, and their humility before him. The unknown writer of the Epistle to Diognetus said, "As the soul is in the body, so are the Christians in the world".

The Christians serve a world which has lost its soul—by the lifting up of their own souls in adoration. (CEA)

TRADITIONAL PRINCIPLES   July 8

There is, I believe, a great tradition of Christian teaching about main principles, drawn from our Lord and the apostles. It calls for interpretation and application in changing circumstances, but it is constant in its main lines.

To give a few instances: the selfish motive in all affairs is always wrong, and the altruistic motive is always right. Wealth is always dangerous to its possessor, and the rich man can only with difficulty be saved. There is no discrimination between races in God's eyes, and there must be no discrimination in man's eyes: the different races share freely in the Church's fellowship.

But it is one thing to state main Christian principles or to denounce a downright evil. It is another thing to commend a particular programme on which the technical skills and wisdom of competent Christians may differ, and to say, "This is the Christian programme", as if to unchurch, or label as second-grade, any Christians who might for good reasons dissent. (CPT)

PRE-POLITICAL PRINCIPLES   July 9

Some of the basic Christian principles I would describe as pre-political rather than political.

For instance, I do not think it can be said that democracy, or majority rule as such, is a Christian principle, and we remember that Christ sometimes showed contempt for the views of majorities.

What *is* a Christian principle, however, is the equal right of every person created in God's image to the full realisation of his powers of mind and body—and this includes full and free citizenship, with democracy as its corollary.

We should always distinguish carefully between a non-Christian conception of the rights of people to do what they like, and a Christian conception of their right to become by God's grace their own truest selves. In this way Christianity endorses and criticises and corrects the ideal of democracy. (CPT)

CHRISTIANITY AND MARXISM   July 10

I don't see a practical fusion of Christianity and Marxism, because the essence of Christianity is a belief in God and in the supernatural, and the essence of Marxism is a view of reality that confines reality to the historical process and includes a rejection of God and the supernatural. I don't think you can have a fusion between two things as opposite as that.

What you can have is a recognition that Communism embodies certain elements in the Christian tradition in isolation from the rest, and that it can also represent certain values that Christianity ought to represent, but doesn't. Thus, while there can't be a fusion of the two, there can be a profitable dialogue between them —which is a different matter.

In answer to a question at the London School of Economics, 1971

AVOID THIS SORT OF INCONSISTENCY   July 11

We must avoid positions which are so inconsistent as to involve a kind of Pharisaism.

We cannot applaud Europeans who resisted the tyranny of a Hitler and then be shocked when Africans want to resist a tyrannical regime today: we can discuss the wisdom or expediency, but we cannot indulge in facile moral censures. We too easily form a habit of exculpating the violence in our own sphere of history, and censuring the violence of other races.

We need to avoid a selective mentality in our moral judgments generally.

There are reasons for our concern about white racism through our own involvement in it. But we need to remember that there are African countries where tribal majorities are unjust to tribal minorities, and where killing and suffering have had appalling dimensions. We need to remember the sufferings, which still continue, of Christians and Jews and others under Communist regimes in eastern Europe. Neither the right eye nor the left eye alone can easily see the whole field of human suffering and moral judgment. (CP)

JUST WAR . . .   July 12

I believe that Christianity does not necessarily demand pacifism. I believe that Christians can encourage and participate in a just war—that is, a war conducted by a state or states against oppression, for the protection of the weak, and for the restoration of justice.

But in order to have a just war it is necessary that there should be some prospect of the outcome being just. That's why, on a world scale, it is very hard to see how today there *could* be a just war, because the result would be indiscriminate destruction.

As for a rebellion or revolution, there can, I believe, be a just revolution or rebellion which Christian people should support. But the condition of its justice must include the prospect that from it there is going to emerge not only the destruction of a bad order, but also the substitution for it of an order that is good and just.

Such conditions are very difficult indeed to foresee, but this is an area in which Christian thought must work out more precisely what *are* the conditions of a just rebellion, bearing in mind that all the conclusions of a just war are not necessarily admirable.

In answer to a question at the London School of Economics, 1971

Through the centuries probably only a minority of considering Christians have held that Christ's teaching demands the totally pacifist position.

I would hold myself that the injunction to turn the other cheek and to offer no resistance to evil—like many other of Christ's injunctions—concerns motive. Faced with a violent attack, the follower of Christ must have total selflessness in motive; so far as his own pride or comfort or security is concerned, he must be ready to accept death, and have no self-concern. But given that selflessness of motive which Christ demands, he may strike, or risk killing, or even kill if his concern is to protect others, whether family, friends, neighbours, enemies, or the community itself.

It has been found possible, however hazardous, to strike in defence of others without hatred, anger, or self-concern. And, conversely, it is possible to be physically passive while bearing anger and hatred.

It is such considerations which cause many conscientious Christians not to endorse total pacifism. (CP)

WAR AND RECONCILIATION   July 14

Suppose there is a just war: Christian people who are members of the Church fight in it. Suppose there is a just rebellion: Christians who are members of the Church fight in that.

But the Church as an organisation, while it says it is right for Christians to do this or that, doesn't take part in belligerent activities, because ultimately the Church's role is a reconciling one.

Suppose Germany oppresses Poland or Holland: the Church can say it is right to resist, and can encourage Christian people to join in the resistance. But the Church doesn't send money to the military organisations because that would be blurring the role of the Church with the role of Christian citizens.

In answer to a question at the London School of Economics, 1971

Hope lies in the existence of Christian men and women who know that these questions about violence and non-violence are crucial for humanity, who do not claim to know all the answers, but are passionately keen to try to find answers which are both intellectually serious and congruous with the Spirit of Christ. (CP)

THIRD-WORLD CHRISTIANITY   July 16
It is difficult to have a share in the wide-ranging work of Christian unity without realising that the focus of Christianity in the world has already become no longer Western or white as regards numbers, and is becoming no longer Western or white in leadership.

And the ethos of the younger Christianity is inevitably different from the ethos of the older. Just as we in the West understand our Christianity through the medium of our Western culture, so inevitably the peoples of the Third World will understand Christianity through the medium of their own concerns. And their concerns are poverty, and the struggle for justice.

"I THOUGHT I WAS A PERSON"   July 17
Paternalism: we need to understand both the big role it has played—not ignobly—in the past, and its obsoleteness today.

In the earlier years of the development of Africa as the unknown continent, the paternalistic spirit of Christian missionaries did a great work, with qualities of love, care for persons, self-sacrifice, and heroism. That is why there are good Christians today in Africa and elsewhere who find it hard to shed the paternalistic assumptions of their own past. We need to understand this.

But while paternalism is understandable as a hangover, it has no future now. As Bishop Muzorewa from Rhodesia said the other day, "They say I am a revolutionary; I thought I was a person".

"I thought I was a person": that is the voice of the future. (CP)

Jesus always appeals to a person in the whole social context of that person's existence. He never appeals to souls in a kind of vacuum.

No person lives in a vacuum. Every person, by being a person, is himself or herself a bundle of human relationships—a father, a son, a wife, a husband, an employed person or an employing person, a member of a village, a town, a city, a business, a community with a hundred involvements—social, political, economic—that are part of the very stuff of life.

And when we talk of someone being converted to Jesus, if it is the real Jesus, then all those relationships that make up a personal being begin to be converted too. And it is at that point that again and again the presentation of Jesus and the response to Jesus have tended to be polarised into two one-sided opposites.

It is possible to present Christianity as a gospel of social improvement for the advancement and liberation of all the conditions of human life, and to do that in such a way that the Gospel is so identified with social betterment that the personal conversion of persons to Jesus Christ as Lord is left out.

Equally it has been possible to present Jesus as Lord, and to try to convert people to him while leaving out that social context that is part of life itself.

CHRISTIANS DON'T KNOW ALL THE ANSWERS   July 19

Christians can practise a wrong kind of otherworldliness and be too ready to show the relevance of religion by dogmatising on subjects which require the touch of an expert as well as the concern of a Christian. (CP)

FORGIVEN AND FORGIVING   July 20

To have been forgiven oneself is the greatest possible impulse towards forgiving others, and the will to forgive others is the test of having effectively received God's forgiveness.

The true Christian is essentially the "forgiven person". It is this characteristic which helps him to be humble towards God, and to serve his fellows without becoming self-assertive or aggressive while he does so.

Lord, take my heart from me, for I cannot give it to thee. Keep it for thyself, for I cannot keep it for thee. And save me in spite of myself. (ICF)

TOLERATION AND CONVICTION   July 21

Toleration means that a man who holds opinions does not want to impose them on others by any external pressure, or enforce them by any means save persuasion. Similarly, a tolerant state will not coerce or punish people for holding particular opinions, and a tolerant religion will not propagate its belief except by winning minds and consciences to accept it.

The definition applies only if a man holds opinions. If a man holds no opinions or convictions, he is not being tolerant if he acquiesces in other people's; he is being indifferent. This needs to be emphasised. Indifference is not toleration; indifference is not a virtue. The indifferent man exercises no self-restraint, no humility, when he says he does not mind the opinions of others.

Today we need to be aware of the distinction. People steeped in the laziness of mental and moral indifference are apt to pride themselves on being tolerant; they are not. Theirs is none of the nobility of those who, with strong and passionate convictions, yet discipline themselves painfully not to trample on the convictions of others; or those who—perhaps with a hard struggle and occasional lapses—combine zeal for a cause with courtesy towards its opponents. (CEA)

TRUE TOLERANCE   July 22

True tolerance implies convictions. The tolerant man, however, reverences the processes by which he reached his own convictions—

the processes of reason, argument, intuition, conscience—and he therefore reverences the same processes at work in another man which lead that man to his own convictions. (CEA)

SCIENTIFIC HUMANISM   July 23

Humanism is a very old phenomenon which flowered wonderfully in the Greek world, and flowered again in the great scholars and writers of the Renaissance. And it has been flowering again in our own time. Humanism essentially means a great reverence for man, for man's dignity, and man's wonderful potentialities.

What is today called scientific humanism is a particular version of humanism, dominated by a faith in the sciences as able to make man competent to solve the problems of human existence, and capable of leading a happy and moral life in society.

Now we, as Christians, are bound to criticise the theses of scientific humanism, because, on the one hand, it does not diagnose properly the depth of man's trouble—that man as a creature is estranged from God his Creator—nor does it look high enough to the real heights of man's potentiality, not just to be a competent, moral, intelligent citizen of this world, but to be a saint reigning with Christ in glory in heaven, with the wonderful glow of humility, and the beauty of saintliness.

So we say that humanism does not see deep enough into the pit of man's predicament, nor high enough into the potentialities of man's glory.

THE TROUBLE WITH MAN   July 24

I refer to the scientific humanist with great respect because as a Christian I share with him a great regard for man, for human dignity, for human worth, and human freedom. I believe that Christians and scientific humanists have much in common in their belief in the dignity of man and the service of mankind. But we part company on this.

The scientific humanist believes that if the knowledge of the sciences develops as it should, and if all the sciences, duly developed, are applied to human affairs in the right way, then the human race can be made more progressive, better organised, more comfortable, more happy, and indeed more moral as well. The scientific humanist will reject religion and the religious dimension altogether, as being an unnecessary drag upon the rightful scientific progress which of itself can put the human race to rights.

My criticism is this: the evidence seems to show that the human race can become increasingly advanced in the knowledge of the sciences and the application of the sciences to human affairs, but can still go on being proud and selfish and cruel and insensitive. The tragic thing is that in the century in which the sciences have made the most stupendous strides, we have also seen the most terrible reactions in mass hysterical cruelty and selfishness.

The scientific humanist's diagnosis does not go deep enough. The trouble with man is not that he is not sufficiently progressive or scientifically enlightened, but that he is too deeply estranged from his Creator, and needs to be reconciled to his Creator in awe and humility—to be cured of his deep pride and selfishness.

CHRISTIAN HUMANISTS   July 25

We have to maintain our critique of humanism. But the humanist values of themselves are good and God-given. Reverence for man, concern for man's freedom, respect for the dignity of man, reverence for man's mind: all these positive features of humanism are things about which it is for us to recognise that God is there in the middle of them as author and giver. The limitations of humanism—no. The false inferences of humanism—no. But the deep values that humanism enshrines can very often set us a good example.

I get very concerned when Christians try to wave a sort of

anti-humanist flag, because if we advance the thesis, "Boo! Christians can't be humanists", we are going to get the counter-thesis, "Well, humanists can't be Christians". I call myself unashamedly a Christian humanist, and invite my fellow Christians so to describe themselves—thus cutting the ground from under what is false in the humanist position, while acknowledging that God is there in the heart of all that is good and beautiful and loving and of good report in the humanist culture.

POST-ESTABLISHMENT   July 26

Looking at the whole stream of Christian history, is it true that Christianity in the world in general is now passing into a post-establishment phase? I think it is, and that we need to be seeing the picture in terms of our own involvement with our fellow Christians in every part of the world, and not only in national terms.

I believe Christian history is passing into a new phase. I think it is likely that the existing Church and State relationship in England will in course of time disappear, and if it does we need have no tremors because the world is full of Churches, including Anglican Churches, which show us how it is possible to be non-established and at the same time healthy, virile, and involved in the service of the community in Christian witness.

Yet I make this caution to the disestablishment camp. I believe that another perhaps more important issue is appearing on the scene. Not the contrast between State Churches and non-State Churches, but the contrast between institutional Christianity—as we have known it in highly organised church structures—and what may be called experimental Christianity—Christian people of real conviction, finding conviction, worship, fellowship, not in a superficial way but in real depth—yet rather loosely related to the old institutional structures.

It must be made clear that the question of being respectable, privileged, and entrenched, and being liberated and suffering with

Christ, does not go *pari passu* with establishment or non-establishment. It is possible to be non-established and yet very respectable and involved in society. There is a kind of worldliness and privilege apparent in non-established forms of Christianity in many parts of the world. None the less, I believe that by and large we are in this new phase, and that our present Church and State relationship in England may be the last of such relations on the globe, and I believe that it will go. But I think it is impossible to force the currents of history, and undesirable to try to do so violently unless we are very sure about what we are getting at.

To the General Synod, 1971

COMFORT IN CATASTROPHE   July 27

The Epistle to the Hebrews was written to give comfort to people dismayed by one of the catastrophes of history—either recent or imminent when the epistle was written—the destruction of the temple in Jerusalem, which had been to so many the symbol of all that made life worth living.

The writer spoke to them of "the removing of those things that are shaken, that the things which are not shaken may remain". Christianity from the first days was organised for catastrophe. Again and again it has witnessed "the removing of those things which are shaken", and no less surely the survival of "the things which are not shaken".

We must expect and we must pray that the presence of the Christian community in the world will make for peace and reconciliation, for the divine leavening of civilisation. But whenever catastrophes seem even possible, then there must be no doubt in the Church's mind as to what are the things chiefly to be hated and dreaded: and what a Christian hates and dreads most is not that the world may end or that we ourselves may go out of it in death, but that any man or woman or child made for fellowship with God the Creator and Father should be separated from him by sin.

That is the priority in a Christian's hate and fear: and with that priority in our hearts we look up to Jesus, our great high priest. He, in every age, whether in peace or calamity, unites human lives to himself in the fellowship of the Church: a kingdom that cannot be shaken, a kingdom embracing us on earth, the souls in paradise, and the saints in heaven.

GOD IS TRULY CHRIST-LIKE   July 28

Jesus is divine: that is the faith of Christendom.

But there is a corollary to it: God is Christlike. Christian people can sometimes in their devotion to Jesus fail to do justice to the corollary: God is Christlike. So it may happen that people feel the appeal of Jesus as "the Man for others", but find the image of God, as we Christians convey it, hard and conventional.

Whenever that happens we are challenged to see to it that our own image of God is truly Christlike. We learn from Jesus what it means, in self-giving love, for God to be God. (ICF)

DIVINE JUDGMENT ON MAN   July 29

"Inasmuch as you did it not to the least one of these, you did it not to me." So speaks Christ to us. Inasmuch, he says, as you neglect the divine image in the other man and do not care about him, you are doing this to me.

The Crucifixion of Jesus stands as the divine judgment upon every man's insensitivity to every man. And we today are living in an hour of divine judgment. The vast increases in civilisation, in culture, in the use of the sciences, in the astonishing development of men's powers, have not eradicated from man his readiness to trample on the rights of others.

So we proclaim the Christian message. Return to God, we say. Return to your Creator and your Saviour.

There is a power not seldom seen in men and women who so bear suffering and so use it that it is turned into something fruitful, creative in love, sympathy, fellowship, saintliness.

It is useless to describe this from without. See the men and women of whom this is true, and try to learn their secret, and then you will begin to grasp the meaning of the words—used sometimes glibly, but in description of a great reality—"redemptive suffering".

It is in Christ supremely that we have seen this: and if Christ is God indeed, there we find the Creator himself dealing with the suffering of his creatures. (ICF)

Since man is in the divine image, and the love of God for each and every member of the human race is infinite, the goal is heaven, which is the perfect fellowship of God's human creatures with himself in glory.

In heaven God's creatures perfectly reflect God's goodness in their selfless service of him and of one another, and enjoy the vision of him and the inexhaustible adventure of knowing, serving and seeing one whose goodness and beauty are perfect.

Heaven is everlasting, and it is the fulfilment of man's meaning as created in the divine image, and of God's infinite love for each and all. Thus heaven gives perspective to man's present existence, and man's life in this world is but a brief prelude to the goal for which he was created. (SS)

AUGUST

TRADITION CAN LIBERATE   August 1

The Church of the living God is the pillar and ground of truth.
It needs to present this truth to successive generations, and in this
cause to adapt its idiom, and to study the needs of particular epochs.

But while successive epochs seem to be so very new, and while
we are apt to dwell on the uniqueness of our own time and its problems, the Church of the living God is a family of saints and a
storehouse of divine gifts and divine wisdom, reaching across the
generations like a colony of heaven in the middle of the flux of
history.

We are apt to be enormously impressed by new wisdom: we are
apt to forget how often it is the timely recovery of some old wisdom
which meets the needs of the moment. Again, we are apt to think
that tradition is inevitably a thing which enslaves and holds in
bondage. In truth, tradition can be a gloriously liberating thing for
us. It frees us from the dominance of some passing fad or fashion or
enthusiasm; it liberates us into a larger realm wherein we are free
from the tyranny of both today and yesterday.

Consider for a moment the Apostles' Creed, the classic document of Christian tradition. It binds us indeed to a pattern of words

and images, but it liberates us from current ideologies into a large perspective wherein saintly men and women of every age have lived in a glorious freedom. (DEA)

CHRISTIAN CLASSICS   August 2

In our preoccupation with the contemporary, it is necessary to remember that it is not only contemporary books which possess relevance and the power to nourish mind and soul.

The priest, in his understanding of people in their contemporary needs and problems, pierces through to the depths of what is timeless and permanent in human need: to the man or the woman as creature and child of an eternal God.

Hence he must equip himself not only with contemporary books, but with those Christian classics whose value and authority reach far beyond particular epochs—St. Augustine, St. Bernard, the Lady Julian of Norwich, Walter Hilton, Baxter, Bunyan, William Law, Newman, Maurice—to cite some of the great names at random.

GOD'S THOUGHTS ARE NOT OUR THOUGHTS   August 3

There are those who, eager to respect the contemporary mind and the claims of reason, try to deny to God anything which seems to be beyond the contemporary grasps or rational comprehension.

To do this is to miss the fact that God's thoughts are not our thoughts, nor God's ways our ways, and that eye has not seen, ear has not heard, nor has it entered into the heart of man to conceive what God has prepared for them that love him.

Such is the God whom we preach. (CPT)

SCIENCE AND TRUTH   August 4

The sciences which flourish within the secular world bear upon the truth concerning God and man wherever they are true in their methods and findings.

146

The lesson of the nineteenth century must not be forgotten. The historic Christian faith found itself confronted by the new sciences of historical criticism and evolutionary biology, and to many those sciences seemed to undermine belief in divine revelation in the Bible, and divine creation of the world and man. It took some years of trial and error to bring the realisation that the new sciences did not undermine but rather enhanced the Christian understanding of the mode of biblical revelation and the wonder of divine creation.

The moral is that God teaches his people not only through sacred theology, but also through sciences often called "secular", and sacred theology is learner as well as mother. It is easy to grasp this moral as we survey a preceding century: it is harder to grasp its relevance to the century in which we are living. (SS)

SCIENCE AND RELIGION   August 5

All science has God as its author and giver. Much is heard of the conflict between science and religion, and of the contrast between sacred and secular. There may be aspects of truth to which religion is the gate, as indeed there are aspects of truth to which particular sciences are the gate. But if there be a Creator, and if truth be one of his attributes, then everything that is true can claim his authorship, and every search for truth can claim his authority.

When science has appeared to be anti-religious it generally has meant that one or two particular sciences were exaggerating their claim to a sort of omnicompetence for reading the whole meaning of the universe, even though one particular science is, of course, not competent to do more than read one particular aspect of the universe.

But the more we Christians are ready to see and acknowledge God in the sciences—God in the truly scientific spirit—the more we shall be witnessing to what is true to the presence of God in the world, and the more entitled we shall be to go on to point out that there can indeed be a certain sort of scientifically trained mentality which is narrow and unperceptive, and robbing itself of a real chance of interpreting the universe aright.

GOD IN THE MIDDLE   August 6

What is sometimes called the conflict between religion and science often proves to be not between religion and science as such, but between bad religion making wrong claims and a bad scientific outlook also making false claims.

A narrow kind of religion that can see God only in biblical literalism, and is blind to the presence of God in the sciences (which, if we could learn from them, would help us to understand the Bible itself better)—that sort of narrowness is a positive invitation to the scientific man to take an anti-religious standpoint, because we are taking a less than truly religious standpoint ourselves in our claim.

We may complain that the scientific mind—by which I think we really mean the technological kind of mind—is very often blind to spiritual values because it practises a sort of omnicompetence which so blinds it.

But we are not now talking about certain sorts of scientific mind, but about the sciences themselves. Take a genuine human science practised with skill and knowledge and integrity. Its author is said to be Mr. So-and-so, or Sir Somebody-Somebody, or Lord Somebody the great biologist, the great geologist, the great astronomer—or whatnot. But the real author of any science is God—the divine Spirit, the Spirit of Truth at work.

It is for us Christians to be far more sensitive to the presence of God in the very middle of all human sciences, and to be more ready to acknowledge God there.

If scientists sometimes are not Christians or believers, we do not help by being blind to God in their work. No, we must all the

148

more acknowledge that God is the author and sustainer of the sciences.

MEN OF SCIENCE   August 7

Robert Boyle, described on his tombstone as the "father of chemistry and the uncle of the Earl of Cork", was said by Gilbert Burnet to have "the profoundest veneration of the great God of Heaven and Earth that I have ever observed in any person". Isaac Newton wrote more about the Bible and the Christian faith than he ever wrote on physical and mathematical science. John Ray found in his studies both a unity and a comprehensiveness reflected in the title, *The Wisdom of God manifested in the Works of Creation.*

It was not that, while being men of science, they happened also to be pious: it was not that, while being men of science, they were clinging to the relics of a faith which, had they been a little more scientific, they would have discarded. Rather was it that in their science they were filled with the sense of "nature" in its old-fashioned meaning: not nature as a particular set of phenomena with a restricted set of instruments for their study, but nature as the study of all that is known, including man himself: man in his achievements of mind and spirit, as well as in his affinity with the animal world.

Nature to those pioneers of science was something which evoked from them awe and wonder, so that the impulse to investigate was one with the impulse to give praise to God.

To the British Association, 1959

POTENTIALITY OF MAN   August 8

As the potentiality of animal life is seen in the remarkable animal called man, so the potentiality of man is seen in him whom the New Testament calls "the New Man", Christ. (CP)

"WHAT IS MAN THAT THOU ART MINDFUL OF HIM?"

August 9

And what indeed is man?

People of many religions or of none, people of many philosophies or of none will join in saying that man is the being of highest significance in the world, and in echoing the old words of Sophocles: "Many things are marvellous, and nothing is more marvellous than man".

Christians, as indeed Jews, have their own belief about this, that man is created by God in God's own image, with fellowship with God for ever as the goal of his existence. God created the human race by an evolutionary process through many stages of nature. He has a care for every one of us, each in his own individuality, a care for each of us so great that it is as if there might be no one else in the world for him to care for. He cares so much for each one that—quite simply—he wants each one to be with him in the perfect fellowship of heaven for ever

If we think rightly about heaven, it is not remote from the concerns of today and tomorrow. Rather it is the supreme assertion of how greatly God cares about every human person today and tomorrow. It is a caring with an eternal significance, and an eternal goal.

THE ARDENT CHRISTIAN

August 10

I thank God for the ardent Christian.

If you are such, be sure now that these are the words that apply to you: "Every branch that beareth fruit, he cleanseth it that it may bear more fruit". Your need is the pruning knife of Christ. Perhaps you are called now to a greater use of the mind in the serious study of your faith. Perhaps it is the taking in hand of prayer in a new way that is the urgent need. Perhaps it is penitence: I should not wonder. Perhaps it is some new practical service for your fellows. Above all, be asking what is the will of Christ for you in the future.

The world is a small place: the far-off is now the very near. *Where* in the world is it that Christ wills you to serve him, and humanity in his name? (ICF)

MORAL CONSCIOUSNESS   August 11

Psychiatry has proved able to aid spirituality and morality by dealing with subconscious conflicts which cause aberrations of behaviour.

But it should be the role of psychiatry not to be a substitute for moral decision, but to enlarge the region of conscious moral decision. It is very misleading to equate psychological harmony with the goal of Christian holiness. (SS)

SEXUAL MORALITY   August 12

Sexual morality is in a mess. Some would say at once that the reason is the decline of religious belief and sanction, since it is with that belief and sanction that morality is bound up. Others would say that, on the contrary, this belief and sanction has been the cause of false repression, neurosis, and unhappiness, and that the contemporary revolt was freeing sex to be the happy, carefree, innocent delight it was meant to be, and was pointing a way to new moral insights.

Here the Christian has to make his response. It is not enough to point to a tradition, or to assert an authority. Christian morality is to be *commended* to reason and conscience. We need, while abhorring evil, to try to analyse where the evil lies, and what are the causes which make for it.

The debris of bad apologetics, false images and narrow moralism must be cleared away. The Christian ethic is not primarily a set of rules and prohibitions: "thou shalt", "thou shalt not". It is not an isolated concentration upon sex, as if fornication were the only grave sin, and chastity the paramount virtue. It is not, again, a

151

hush-hush smugness which cannot talk of sex, and leaves it to be deemed unclean or smutty. Nor is it a thing called "sex ethics", invoked to counteract "sex licence", for the essence of the Christian view is that sex is to be understood only in the context of the whole relation of man and woman. (CEA)

... I incurred a lot of abuse from people for contending very strongly for the alteration in the law whereby homosexual acts between adults should not be criminal. But it is one thing to say that something is not criminal, but quite another thing to equate homosexuals' behaviour with marriage—an institution which the Church blesses. I would not agree to the equation of those things for a moment.

THE WORST SIN   August 13

Asked by David Frost in a television interview what was the worst sin of all, the Archbishop replied:

Pride. Not because it is the most blameworthy, but because it is the characteristic sin, the root sin. Pride is the bolstering up of one's own ego; it is the proud person who is unteachable.

A PLACE FOR CONFESSION   August 14

In the Anglican tradition there has always been a place for confession, absolution, and spiritual counsel.

Since the Reformation there has never been a time when there were not many Anglicans who have used the discipline of private confession and absolution, and, in connection with it, have sought a spiritual counsel. But there has been a certain reserve and a refraining from treating it as obligatory and compulsory for all. So it is.

I would say today that there are a great many Anglicans to whom it would do a world of good to go to confession, and yet they don't go. Yet we are glad that the system is voluntary, and that it is not pressed, because of a great principle which the first Queen Elizabeth once enunciated: "We do not open windows into men's souls".

If people like to disclose their souls because they are led to, well and good. But the Church does not use a kind of corkscrew to go probing into people's souls to find what is there, unless the people themselves disclose it to men as well as to God.

LONGING FOR GOD   August 15

We see a Christian who desires God very much. He finds it hard to meditate and think with the mind about God because the mind is feeble and scatterbrained. He may find it hard to pray intelligently for this or that person or for this or that cause, and is very conscious of weakness and inadequacy. But in the very acknowledgement of weakness, inadequacy, and inability to pray, there is a deep longing for God. He wants God very much; he is hungry and thirsty for God, and perhaps all he is able to tell God is that he has a hunger and thirst for him, though even that is very feeble, but he wishes that the hunger and thirst were more.

And this longing for God, when released in simplicity, appears to be, not something that the brain is doing, but rather something in the depths of the person—call it the personality, or the self, or the soul: call it what you will. A writer, Father Augustine Baker, spoke of this longing as the prayer that comes "from the ground of the soul". Well, this hungry longing for God leads on to an experience in which the self—emptying itself of its own capacities— finds itself filled by God. (SS)

TOGETHER WITH GOD   August 16

How do we soak ourselves in God's heart and mind? It is like the overwhelming impact of person upon person when two are together, listening, loving, pondering, assimilating.

153

Now this can be put into religious language, the language of psalm and hymn and devotion. Perhaps you find that language unreal to you, and are shy of it. Very well, do not force yourself into it. And yet there may be ways in which, haltingly, inarticulately, you find God real to you, in the sense of supreme moral obligation which you sometimes feel; or in the reverence of lovely qualities in people which seem to be somehow beyond, and to give meaning to, human existence; or in the sense of wonder at the world and its meaning.

There you find the reality which has the name of God. But just because he is supreme and majestic and you are not, it is not you finding him so much as he finding you.

"Before I sought thee, thou didst find me." (MP)

FINDING THE REAL JESUS   August 17

Is Jesus real to you? There was his historical life which the Gospels describe. There is his existence now, risen from the dead. If you want him to be more real to you than you feel just now, you can do far more to let him be so. There is the gospel, and there is the sacrament.

Look at the Gospel of St. John. I suggest it because, more than any other book, it shows Jesus as he was in history, together with Jesus as he is in his universal, timeless appeal. Read from—say—chapter 13 onwards, about the last deeds and words of Jesus before his death. Here is a little work for you in the next few days. It will help Jesus to be real to you.

Jesus still gives himself to us: he does this so that the relationship ceases to be external, like the relation of you and someone standing near you: it becomes the relationship described in the words, "I am the vine, ye are the branches. Dwell in me, and I in you".

How? First, by the word of Jesus. That means that, when you read his teaching, as in the chapters I have suggested, you not only use your mind: you use imagination, and affection, and will. You let what you read become meat and drink to you.

Second, by the sacrament of Holy Communion. It is *broken* body, blood *poured* or *offered*, that we receive as the food of our souls. Broken. Offered. It is the same divine self-giving of which we have been thinking, self-giving right down to death. That is the answer to our pride, and to the world's frustration.

Thus, by Word and Sacrament, Jesus has his impact upon human lives today. It is the impact which St. John describes in "the Word became flesh, and dwelt among us: and we beheld his glory ... full of grace and truth". *Glory* is one of the great words of the Christian vocabulary. It means here the self-giving love seen in Jesus, the very opposite of the human glory of self-esteem or the esteem of men. *Grace* is the power whereby Jesus makes us different. *Truth* is all that he shows us about God, the world, and ourselves. (ICF)

TEST OF REALITY   August 18

The Eucharist is the heart of the Church's life. It also happens in the middle of this created world with all its realities and tensions and sufferings.

So we do not receive communion as living in a vacuum. We plead Christ's sacrifice; we offer ourselves on behalf of the world around us, and the reality of our offering is tested by the genuineness of our care for our neighbours, and our will to serve the community with the love which flows from Christ crucified.

Is this real? Does this happen? If you go about this country from parish to parish, you will find parishes which seem lifeless: the worship is formal, the worshippers are like separate units; fellowship, social conscience, care for the world, seem far away. Go to others: there is true fellowship, otherworldly and practical—both; there is an outgoing force in mission and in service.

And you? Wherever you are, help Christian worship to be what it is meant to be by being what a Christian is meant to be. (ICF)

"UNDER" CHRIST   August 19

Clearly, then, being a Christian does not mean being "for" Christianity, and "against" the non-Christians, or "for" Christ like a cause or movement to which you give approval.

It means being one who belongs to Christ, as putting yourself "under" Christ. It means being one who asks Christ to rule heart and will, so that you are free for possibilities you would otherwise never be free for. It means being one who uses obediently those means of union with Christ which Christ has given. It means being one who accepts Christ's pruning knife, and so learns to be humble.

There are some who consciously offer self to God. There are others who forget self altogether in serving God and others. If a man must be aware of himself, it is a happy thing if he can *laugh at himself*, for that is a way of coming near to God.

Less of self, more of Christ: that is the proof of what we believe. Even so, come Lord Jesus. (ICF)

THE BACKGROUND   August 20

Now for the Old Testament. Jesus Christ did not live and teach in a vacuum. He came to a people who had already been trained to know the God of Moses, Amos, Hosea, Isaiah, and the Psalmists; and their God was his own God too. We do not understand Jesus apart from this background of Israel's history and Israel's faith. He brought the faith to its climax, he gave the full and final revelation of the God whom the prophets and the psalmists had made known incompletely. But they still matter greatly, as they prepare the way for Jesus, both witnessing to him, and even now helping to lead us to him.

How varied are the books of the Old Testament: history, chronicle, poems, dramas, tales. But they all tell of the chosen people, and of the God who is making himself known to them.

We need not set limits to the media which God can use in making his truth known. Literal fact and history are not the only ones; drama, myth, and symbols are others, as God speaks to our imagination as well as to our literal little minds.

"RELIGION OF A BOOK" August 21

There have been inevitable drawbacks accompanying the idea of a "sacred volume" or the "religion of a book". It has been all too possible for Christians to use the Old Testament and the New Testament as a single corpus of inspired scripture so as to interpret the latter in a kind of subservience to the former, and even perversely to reverse their true relationship.

It has also been possible to use the New Testament writings as a kind of uniform textbook, and to miss the creative dynamism of the histories and personalities which went into its making.

Worst of all, it has been possible to see biblical revelation not as the witness of writers to Jesus Christ, but as a chain of things which "the Bible says". Thus the Bible says: Jesus is the Son of God; Jonah was three days and three nights in the belly of the whale; it is a shame for a man to have long hair; it is not permitted for a woman to speak in the assembly. It gives them all the same authority.

It is not only that such literalism has again and again loomed large in the Church's use of the Bible. It is also that, even where literalism has been avoided, the idea that the Bible is a corpus of revelatory statements has been present, if not in the consciousness at least in the subconsciousness, of probably every Christian community through the centuries.

Revelation has been seen as the contents of a book, rather than as the dynamic process of persons, events, and witness, which brought the book into existence. (CP)

If we come closer to the inner heart of Bible reading we are not just stuffing our minds with information; we are letting God feed us through his word, and this means letting the scriptures speak to imagination, conscience, feeling, and will, as well as to the mind.

As we read, and read slowly, we pause and let the truth of God come home to us. Our imagination is moved to *wonder*, our conscience is pricked to *penitence*, our feelings are moved to *love*, our will is stirred to *resolve*, and our mind to whatever *understanding* we can muster.

In that way we quietly let the passage of scripture come home to us, mould us, and be our food and drink.

INTERRUPTIONS   August 23

Our faithfulness is again and again tested by our power to deal with interruptions. You plan your day according to some rule, with so many hours for this, and so many for that; then all seems thrown into disorder by interruptions. You fail to do all that you set out to do, and you may get hot and bothered and feel that what you planned as order has turned to chaos.

But think of it in terms of the will of God. If the will of God is that you should accept this or that interruption and you accept it with gladness, then a day which might seem tempestuous is really filled with plan and peace and order. For where the will of God is, there is God's presence and God's peace. And where that will is obeyed, there is pattern and harmony.

In his will is your peace. (CPT)

THE NEWS   August 24

"And David said, 'How went the matter? I pray thee, tell me.'"

The messenger ran from the battlefield to King David and told him the news. A great victory had been won, but Saul and Jonathan were dead. And David was very moved, and he broke into poetry, and sang one of the great songs of all time: "Thy glory is slain in high places, how are the mighty fallen".

That was news. News is the communication of an event. Any event of itself is sterile: it is when it is communicated that it has its effects, whether on the world or on the few human lives most concerned, or on human emotions of gladness or grief. What a role then is played by anyone who carries news—in speech, or in writing. He stands between the events and the results of the event. He helps to make history.

It is a precious right to publish news freely. It is a right which sometimes has had to be fought for; and its existence is now a part of our civilisation: the right to record events, and the right to comment upon them.

"How went the matter? I pray thee, tell me."

To the Press Association

ALL NEWS IS ABOUT PEOPLE   August 25

We who are not members of the Press do well to reflect sometimes on the qualities of brain and character which the work of the Press calls for; to pick up events, sometimes very rapidly and yet accurately; to probe into the value of bits of evidence which may present themselves, to get the context and perspective right, to communicate the result to the receiving end, and all the time to keep the human relations necessary for every point in the enterprise—for all news is about people, and is communicated to people.

In Fleet Street as a whole there is, day by day, an amazing technological skill: there is the human fellowship which alone can get things done by concerted efforts, and there is a host of human links around the world. And all this is done for the purpose of doing for our modern world what was done by the messenger when

King David asked, "How went the matter? I pray thee, tell me."

To do the work of the Press at all needs brains and character; to do the work as well as it can be done needs something beyond merely human capacities. To stand between events and their communication, to stand between events and their results—it is a stupendous responsibility, and there is something awesome about it.

How much is at stake for the world in this, and how much also is at stake for the happiness of the men, women, and children concerned in any event which brings joy or sorrow! To speak of this issue is to be on the frontier of things human and things divine. And Christians believe that all news is of concern to God, our Creator and our Judge, because the greatest news of all was the news the shepherds carried, running from the stable at Bethlehem; the news that the women carried, running from the tomb on Easter morning; the news the evangelists have written to be read until the end of time.

For all of us who make news, and communicate news, and read news, let there be the simplicity of purpose in the old words of David: "How went the matter? I pray thee, tell me".

To the Press Association

LOVE FOR LANGUAGE August 26

There must be a recovery of love for language among those who speak and write in the Church's name. The role of language was well described by Bishop Westcott: "A great society cannot exist without great ideas; and great ideas cannot exist without worthy utterance".

A prayer written or chosen for a particular occasion is not good enough unless it can survive to be valued on other occasions too. A document deserves oblivion unless it is clearly and incisively written. I am pleading for nothing highbrow, precious, academic. Far from it. I am pleading that when words are used in the service of religion, there should be a care and love for them no less than a care and a love for the truth itself.

THE APPEAL TO REASON   August 27

What does the appeal to reason mean as an Anglican characteristic? It is a readiness always to be asking what the Christian faith means in contemporary terms, and to be finding how we can translate it into the intellectual language that our contemporaries are using.

I believe that in every era of Anglicanism, Anglicans have tried to do that. It sometimes has the danger of corrupting the Christian faith through succumbing to misleading tendencies, but it is by that constant duty of contemporary interpretation that the authoritative message is seen in a meaningful and dynamic way.

Another aspect of the appeal to reason is the readiness to go on through the use of scholarship to get a better understanding of things already believed. Let me give two instances. One is the doctrine of scripture itself: we believe in the supreme authority of scripture, just as the men of the sixteenth century did; but we do not understand authority in the same way. We do not use the scriptures in the same way. It is the use of reason through critical scholarship which enables us to have fresh understanding of, and fresh ways of expressing, an old unchanging truth.

The other instance is the doctrine of the Eucharist. I think it is now apparent that in the eucharistic controversies of the sixteenth century there were many issues falsely stated. The issues were obscured by wrong and insufficiently primitive presuppositions. And modern scholarship, studying eucharistic doctrine, has been able to go behind sixteenth-century controversies, and formulate the issues in a new and fresh way. That means that the appeal to scripture and primitive tradition still stands, but our knowledge and

understanding of what scripture and tradition mean can greatly
grow through the use of reason.

ANGLICAN WEAKNESSES   August 28
Just now, traditional Anglicanism is meeting the pressures of the
immense cultural changes of our time, and some of its weaknesses
are becoming apparent.

One weakness is verbosity. Not, I think, that the language is
archaic so much as that there is too much of it; too many adjectives
attached to the same noun. You know what I mean. And I think it
is possible that rites such as the Scottish and American are even
more verbose in that way than the English.

A second defect is that the old Anglican forms have in them too
much of our exhortation element; the bringing into services of
those little sermonettes for the edification of the people. And even
where in the services those sermonettes do not actually occur, there
is a kind of hortatory tone very often brought into the structure
and into the prayers.

Then a third weakness is that the Anglican forms presuppose a
certain kind of intellectual culture, and they make demands on the
mind in following the words and applying the words. And, perhaps
characteristically, while the intellectual element is strong, the affective element of the soul reaching out in affection towards God is
rather underemphasised. I think you know what I mean—those acts
of love towards God, coming from the heart and soul, rather than
from the mind.

THE IDEA OF THE HOLY   August 29
The idea of the holy in Christianity is, through and through, a
matter of persons. The immense concern of the modern world for
persons challenges us to strip the idea of the holy to personal realities. The religious man will then be sure that the Godwardness to
which he is called is to be found and practised in and through the

thousands of decisions which constitute his being a person. And he will meet the numinous, and reverence it, not only in the religious God–man relationship, but within the ups and downs of human life.

It is within human life, and indeed within the non-religious aspects of human life, that many of the phenomena which we call transcendence occur. Transcendence is seen in human actions which are terrifying in generosity, in forgiveness, in self-giving, in acts of selfless identification with human misery. Here is seen *mysterium tremendum et fascinans* (a mystery which frightens and attracts), a beyondness which tells of another world.

We can pray only in the world, through the world, as ourselves part of the world, and there is no love for God within which the world is not included. We are, in a sense, never apart from the world. But we need to go apart from its preoccupation, its pressure and its noise, in order to be open to our freedom as sons and creatures of God eternal.

The contemplation of God—and contemplative prayer is, I believe, not necessarily an advanced state, but something accessible to us backward Christians—the waiting upon God in quietness can be our greatest service to the world if in our apartness the love for people is in our heart.

As Aaron went into the holy of holies wearing a breastplate with jewels representing the twelve tribes of Israel upon it, so the Christian puts himself deliberately into the presence of God with the needs and sorrows of humanity upon his heart. And he does this best, not by the vocal skill with which he informs the Deity about the world's needs, but by the simplicity of his own exposure to God's greatness and the world's need.

FOR ORDINARY CHRISTIANS   August 30

In modern times in our Anglican Church, as well as in Catholic spirituality in Europe, there came about a tendency to regard discursive meditation (called by whatever name) as a norm for most Christians, and to think of any approach to contemplative prayer as a thing far removed, and characteristic of advanced souls or mystics. But we have seen the recovery of an older tradition of spirituality, whereby elementary contemplation has a place not only for advanced souls, but for ordinary Christians, too.

This older tradition is beautifully described by Dom Cuthbert Butler, a former Abbot of the Benedictine Monastery of Downside, in his book, *Western Mysticism*. I would myself humbly dare to say that, whereas discursive meditation can become all too easily a cerebral process, putting too much strain upon the powers of the mind, affective prayer, or elementary contemplation, is God's gift to the many who reach out to him in their poverty, their want, their childlike desire.

It is a prayer which some writers describe as coming "from the ground of the soul". I believe the capacity of the ordinary Christian for contemplation is greater by far than some of our theories of spiritual life have allowed. (CEA)

MYSTICISM August 31

Mysticism in the proper sense is an intense realisation of God within the self, and the self embraced within God in vivid nearness.

It is a phenomenon known in a number of religions, and in those religions very similar language is used in describing the experience. There is deep darkness, the darkness of not knowing, and there is light, with flashes in which the self knows the unknowable to be terribly near, and knows itself as never before.

Now, through the centuries Christian teaching has emphasised that the significant thing is not just the mystic experience in itself, but its place and context within the whole life of a Christian. The experience is given by God sometimes to one who seeks God in a life of humility and charity, turned towards righteousness as well as the beauty of God. And the effect of the experience of mystic union, sometimes described as "passive contemplation", is not to cause the person to long to have the experience again, but to long to serve God, and to do his will.

Those who have had mystic experience will not want to tell everyone about it: they will have a longing to serve God in daily life, for in his *will* is our peace. (CP)

SEPTEMBER

VOCATION   September 1

There is in the ordained ministry a distinctive relation to Christ.
All vocations are from God; all alike involve a call to be Christ-like;
all are equally sacred; but the minister of word and sacrament
shares in Christ's own ministry as apostle and shepherd. In the
last resort the call is not to a profession, but to *him*, and men who
are untouched by an ecclesiasticism which dwells upon "the
Church's need" are won by an evangelical realisation of Christ
summoning them to be with him in his work as a shepherd of
souls.

Yet the ways in which this call comes home, and the motives
which draw a man towards it, may be very many. It may work
through stages of attitude and ideal at all sorts of levels, not all of
them pious or orthodox in the least. The ideal of service as a thing
nobler than the claims of selfish ambition has been a motive which
has helped many on their way. Yet ambition itself can help, and
is by no means always an evil. I feel that in parts of our Durham
population the enemy is an attitude of spiritless inclination to live
in a rut, with no ambition after knowledge, education, success,
achievement of any kind. In such conditions, to have *any* ambition

betokens an adventure of the will, and an enlarged awareness of human possibilities.

So, many are the levels on which the mysterious divine process works, until it finds itself in the terms which Hensley Henson used in a memorable letter of his Barking days to a brother Fellow of All Souls: "In ordination I see nothing less than that supreme acceptance of Christ's proposal". (DEA)

A SIGN OF THE MINISTRY   September 2

The priest displays in his own person that total response to Christ to which all members of the Church are pledged. He is to be a beacon of the Church's pastoral, prophetic, and priestly concern. "By ordination a Christian becomes a sign of the ministry of Jesus Christ in his Church".

Besides displaying the Church's response, the priest also enables it, for by his professional training and concentration of labour he gets things done.

And besides displaying and enabling, he also involves the whole Church in his own activity. When he visits a sick person, for instance, it is not only the visit of a kind Christian; it is the Church visiting. Similarly, the priest can be the Church praying, the Church caring for the distressed, the Church preaching.

In the Church, and for the Church, he displays, he enables, he involves. (CPT)

A LEARNED CLERGY   September 3

It is not given to every priest to be learned in the sense of amassing stores of factual knowledge, or of pursuing original research and investigation. He is not necessarily to be learned as the word is commonly used in secular usage. But he *is* called to be learned in the sense of being one who constantly wins fresh knowledge and fresh understanding of the faith which he teaches.

We teach, for instance, of God the Creator, of the Incarnation of the Son, of the mystery of the Cross, of the work of the Holy Spirit;

and it matters greatly that our mind and our imagination are, through constant searching and reflection, being quickened to freshness of grasp and wonder. In this sense there is no priest who cannot be learned, and the promises in the ordination service pledge him so to be.

"Take heed to thy teaching." Make friends with the greatest writers, in biblical exposition, in Christian doctrine, in the classics of Christian spirituality.

Here is one rule within the reach of the busiest curate, and the busiest bishop: to make a special study of one book of the Bible every year. (DEA)

"TAKE HEED TO THYSELF"   September 4

Know yourself, with your idols and your failures exposed in the presence of a Creator who made you for himself, and who sees, below the idols and failures, your longing for him.

And likewise in the years that follow, "take heed to thyself" again, deliberately, regularly. It will not be easy. Not only will the round of ceaseless business in church and parish hinder you, but also (here is the more subtle danger) the devoted practice of prayer and office and penitence can themselves be twisted into a sort of busy-ness which can hide you from yourself in an aroma of professional piety.

So the need is for spaces of quietness, in which you see yourself as you are in the presence of the Creator who made you, and the Lord who ordained you. Take heed to thyself, that self which can deceive itself unless it is revealed in naked simplicity before its God.

It is in this taking heed that a true devoutness—simple, generous, Godward—has its root and its renewing. (DEA)

THE PRESSURES ON THE MODERN PRIEST   September 5

Powerful currents of thought have their effects on the course which the modern priest tries to steer.

On the one side, the quest of religion in the secular, and the reaction from an otherworldly pietism, are questioning the traditional concept of the priest as a man of prayer. The democratic trends within, as well as without, the Church conflict with traditional concepts of the priest's authority. The hunger for "reinterpretation" can erode the integrity of the Gospel as presented in the old scriptural categories.

On the other side, however, are the conservative trends: back to the Bible, back to literalism, back to the supernatural, and let "liberal" be a dirty word. There is also the contrast between those who would preach a gospel of salvation devoid of any social content or context, and those who would identify the gospel with a horizontal programme of social activism.

Among the pressures of these influences upon his thought and feeling, the priest often has too few facilities for study, a dearth of intellectual and spiritual counsel, and anxieties of home and economy to try his spirit. Nothing is more needed than sabbatical periods for rest and intellectual and spiritual refreshment. And no reform is more urgent than that the many tinkerings with this need should give place to a radical plan for meeting it. (CPT)

THE BISHOP   September 6

The bishop is the shepherd, the teacher, the intercessor, in the flock of Christ. He has before him the pattern of our Lord himself. He sees day by day Jesus the Good Shepherd who gave his life for his flock, Jesus the bringer of divine truth who says, "Everyone that is of the truth hears my voice", Jesus who on earth was found a great while before day praying in a desert place apart, and now lives forever to make intercession for us.

As shepherd, the bishop finds it his joyful duty to care especially for the clergy in their care for the parishes, and to bring the means of grace to the people in his own sacramental acts. As teacher, the bishop will not necessarily be a man of speculation and research, but one who brings home with clarity and conviction the faith of the scriptures and the creeds. As intercessor, he is one who goes apart with God on behalf of the people.

Aaron entered the holy of holies with the names of the twelve tribes of Israel engraved upon his breastplate; so the bishop lifts his heart to God with the needs, the sins, and the sorrows of his people graven upon it. Thus does he set before himself Christ—shepherd, teacher, priest. (CEA)

SOCIETY OF SAINTS   September 7

The Church is the society of those who are called to be saints.

In the New Testament all members of the Church are described as saints: the saints in Corinth, the saints in Rome, and so on. They were all brought by baptism into the family of Christ, and received the Holy Spirit, the Spirit of saintliness, to be used or to be quenched by their subsequent response to their calling.

As the Church grows and moves across the globe, and down the centuries of history, its members have inevitably a complex existence. They belong to this divine society, with standards separate from the world's. They belong also to countries, to civilisations, to the world's organised life. Hence backslidings and compromises, and an immense variety among the Church's members. It includes those who try hard, with a patience and a humility which shines through their weaknesses. It includes those who have ceased to try, and whose membership is merely formal. (ICF)

HISSING AND REPROACH   September 8

I know that the Church repels. You look at some of its members and you see complacency, censoriousness, division, vacillating leadership. I feel that too, for I don't live in a sort of haze of purple! I see and I feel the defects of the Church acutely.

Now, it is a very old problem. Israel was chosen by God to

represent his purpose in the world, and Israel sometimes became, in the scathing words of a prophet, "a hissing and a reproach". When Israel failed, judgment fell upon her as upon other nations, and God raised from her a "remnant" and used that remnant for the renewal of his purpose through Israel. There was *scandal*—in the failure of Israel's members, which caused her to be a "hissing". There was *glory*—in the unshaken purpose of God to use Israel for the showing of himself to the world, despite the obstacles they put in the way. And show himself he did, in Israel, through Israel.

So, too, with the Church of the new covenant. Don't shut your eyes to scandal, or your ears to hissing. But have them open to the glory, and it is the glory of Christ in his saints. If you want to be a Christian, you have your duty to the scandal and the glory—both. (ICF)

PURGINGS AND PRIGS   September 9

History shows that attempts to be rid of the scandal of the Church, by puritanically turning out people who don't conform to certain moral standards, cause more evils than they cure.

The Church is a mixed society of those called to be saints, baptised in the Spirit and with very, very mixed responses to it. Yet again and again the sense of the scandal of the Church having so many passengers has led to movements—ancient, medieval, post-reformation—which have said in effect, "Let's turn out of the Church people who don't conform to certain high moral standards". Usually it has taken the form of turning out the fornicators, turning out anybody who has lapsed in respect of sexual morality, and defining the Church as a coterie of those who really do live up to a certain standard.

Attempts to purge the Church like that break down because it is so easy to turn out those who by their actions have failed to uphold those standards, while leaving inside the Church the smug people, the proud people, the prigs and the hypocrites. The Christian

Church was never meant to be a Society of the Moral, but rather a Society of the Forgiven, and of those who put themselves in the way of divine forgiveness; a society ready to carry within its embrace many who have fatally compromised, and all who are unworthy—for all of us are unworthy: the mixed society of those called to be saints.

IF ONLY . . .   September 10

If only the Christian prophets would prophesy, and if only the Christian statesmen would be more wise and courageous!

That is your longing. But the body of the whole Church is one with all its members. And it is when the members generally do *their* bit that the whole Church is nearer to the divine voice, and the prophets and the statesmen are helped to do *their* bit.

If you agree, then your own part is first to be putting yourself nearer to God's will for you in that little realm which you yourself control. It is not only a matter of the causes which you support, of the protests which you make against the evils of society. It is also a matter of what you *do* yourself in the service of God and humanity, and it is, no less, a matter of what you *are* in your immediate relationships to people and to God.

There you will ask God to show you your own share in the world's estrangement from him. *There* you will ask God to forgive you and set you free to make your will the reflection of his own.

"Lord, take my heart from me, for I cannot give it to thee. Keep it for thyself, for I cannot keep it for thee. And save me in spite of myself." (ICF)

CONCERNING LEADERSHIP   September 11

"It's a pity that the leaders of the Church are so rotten." Yes, indeed. It is a worse pity that, when leaders are picked, there is only you to pick them from!

But what is the leadership which the human race needs? It is the leading of the human race into fellowship with the Creator, so as to reflect him in all human affairs. This leadership is the role of the *whole* Christian Church. "As the soul is in the body, so are the Christians in the world."

Within the Church, this leadership is shared by different people in different roles. There are the prophets. God raises them up with particular insight into the divine will and purpose in human affairs. The prophet has eyes which see what the rest of us do not see.

There are statesmen. These are practical people with the gift of carrying out particular implications of the divine will in this or that situation.

There are all the members of the Church. They all share in the task of leading the human race the right way; of healing that derangement of the relation of creatures to their Creator by which humanity is poisoned. Each will look to his or her own share in that derangement.

What is it in *me* that must be put right? (ICF)

DAMAGE   September 12

If you were the Archbishop of Canterbury, anything silly or wicked that you did would do a great deal of damage to the witness of the Christian Church. The people outside the Church would say—as of course they do say—"Look at the old fraud, supposed to be representing Christ and Christianity. We don't think much of that". And those inside the Church would be saying—as they do say—"There you are, he's let us down again; no real leadership, no example for us to follow". No, that's what would happen if you were the Archbishop of Canterbury, and your folly and your sin would do big, culpable, public damage to the Christian Church, and the Christian cause.

But if you are not the Archbishop of Canterbury, then be very sure that you, by your folly and your sinfulness, and your unworthiness as a Christian, can be doing Christ, the Church, yourself, and the Christian cause, just as much great damage.

VICTORY OVER SINFULNESS   September 13

The Christian Church has for centuries portrayed the Cross with the symbols of royalty, majesty, victory. Pictures and statues show Christ crucified, but robed and crowned like a king. Poetry has described the scene on Calvary as a victorious battle. Is this a fancy picture, belonging to the realm of escapist ecclesiastical phantasy?

No. It is a picture of something very real and practical. St. John, in his Gospel, uses the word "glory" of the divine splendour seen in the life of Jesus, and specially seen in his suffering and death. The divine glory is the *self-giving* love, in God eternally, in the Incarnation, and in the death of Jesus.

Opposed to this divine glory of self-giving love is the glory of man in his pride and self-centredness. What can destroy this glory of pride and self-centredness? Only its opposite—by replacing it with the glory of self-giving love.

This is what happens. The glory that was in Jesus when he gave himself even to death is now, in virtue of Jesus being risen and living, reproduced in those who receive and possess his spirit. Christ's self-giving, Christ's death *in you*: Christ's glory therefore *in you*. Is that hard to grasp? It is the very meaning of Christian life. (ICF)

MIRACLES AND FAILURE   September 14

To the General Synod, 3 May 1972, moving the resolution "That the 1968 Scheme for Unity with the Methodist Church be finally approved".

I am told that if this resolution passes with sufficient authority, it will be a miracle. I pray for this miracle, but miracles can be very frightening. And I should be very frightened of this miracle happening unless there is to be another miracle for which we can all pray together: that whether today we say "Yes" or "No", we may all be given a mutual forbearance, a humility before God of a frankly beyond-this-world kind. And in that humility we may know more than ever that our little earthen vessels, with our so-called successes or so-called failures, are not what makes the Church of God.

Come what may, Christ the Lord of the Church reigns, and something which may loom very large at any moment in our consciousness is a tiny little incident in Christ's empire in human lives, which is what the Church means . . .

CLOSING THE DEBATE

. . . Today's discussion leaves me thinking that "Yes" is still the right answer. But I want to end with a word about what happens if "No" is the answer.

If "No" turns out to be the answer, we shall all need a new look at the way to Christian unity. A totally new look: and by "new" I mean a look in which the outcome of what we are going to think we should do is, to begin with, frankly unpredictable; I mean a vacuum in the divine, theological sense, in which we really humbly put ourselves in the hands of God, just not knowing. I believe that will be the only possible way.

In what I would call the humble vacuum, we may be given new insights of a quite unpredictable kind, new powers to learn from one another, new powers to learn very humbly from new Churches —and I think we Anglicans have something to learn about humility towards other parts of Christendom. But for God's sake let us avoid the kind of Pelagianism which says, "This did not work. Now we are going to try to make something else work". We are going to do nothing at all. We are just in the darkness of God's hands. And that darkness which we acknowledge to be darkness can become his new kind of light coming to us.

So I pray for "Yes", but if it be "No", pray forgive me for reading again the sentence I used at the beginning this morning: "Come what may, Christ the Lord of the Church reigns, and something which may loom very large at any moment in our consciousness is a tiny little incident in Christ's empire in human lives, which is what the Church means".

In a word, Long live God! Long live God!

The motion was narrowly defeated

PEOPLE OF THE PRAYER BOOK   September 15

Anglican theology is not confessionalist in the sense in which Lutheran and Calvinist Churches are confessionalist, because it holds together a Confession of Faith with a Book of Common Prayer. And that is very important.

Ask what the position of the Lutheran Church is, and they show you the *Confessio Augustana*; ask what the doctrine of the Kirk of Scotland is, and they show you the Westminster Confession; ask the various Calvinistic professions what their positions are, and they similarly show you Confessions. Ask Anglicans what their position is, and they show you the Thirty-nine Articles—some of them rather wobbly—but bound up with the Book of Common Prayer.

It is this linking of the formulation of dogma with the way of prayer which is supremely characteristic of Anglicanism. So when we Anglicans explain what we stand for to other people, we say to them not just "Come and read our documents; come and argue about theology with us", but "Come and pray with us; come and worship with us". It is that which is characteristic, and it is that that some other Christian confessions have found very hard to understand.

APPEAL TO TRADITION   September 16

The nature of the Anglican appeal to tradition has somewhat shifted through the ages. Anglicans no longer regard it as an appeal to the writings of the Fathers in themselves, so much as an appeal to the continuing life and experience of the worshipping Church. It is as if to say that if we want to read the scriptures so as to understand them with the mind of Christ, we must school ourselves in the common life, witness, and worship of the continuing Christian community; and it is as we live and witness and pray within the life of this community that our hearts and minds are attuned to the right understanding of what the scriptures teach.

We avoid any idea that tradition is a kind of body of truth additional to scripture, to be placed on a pedestal behind it. We think rather of tradition as the living stream of divine truth in the Church, a stream of which scripture itself is the purest and most authoritative part.

In contemporary theology, it would now appear that the old controversies about scripture and tradition are being seen in a very new light, and that Roman Catholics, Anglicans, and Nonconformists are beginning to go behind the old conflicts about scripture and tradition and to see their relationship in the way I have very briefly and inadequately described.

GOD'S SURPRISES   September 17

Resurrection is a mighty act of God. Remember that in the New Testament the language used is not of Jesus rising, but of Jesus being raised by God. Jesus did not "achieve" resurrection: rather did he make himself naught, and when all was dark, when human possibilities were exhausted, God raised him by a mighty act of his power.

This truth about resurrection colours the whole process of man's movements towards his goal, whether in this world or the next. It is not that man, even under God's grace, gets gradually better and better, and so attains to saintliness here, and to heaven hereafter. Rather does the grace of God work surprises, turning defeats into deliverances, "calling things that are naught as though they

178

are", and acting beyond any laws of progress or expectation. (CEA)

GOOD THINGS FOR THEIR OWN SAKE   September 18

No part of early church history is more moving than the questions which St. Augustine sent to Pope Gregory about some of his perplexities, and the answers which the Pope gave him.

One of the matters which bothered St. Augustine was the variety of customs in the different Churches, and Pope Gregory told him that if he found anything in the Gallican or the Roman or in any other Church acceptable to almighty God, he should accept it in England because—and here comes the great principle—"things are not to be loved for the sake of places, but places for the sake of good things". *Non pro locis res, sed pro bonis rebus loca amanda sunt.*

How suggestive, how far-reaching, is this principle; how applicable to other issues and other times! "*Non pro locis res, sed pro bonis rebus loca amanda sunt.*" The local, the limited, the particular, is to be cherished by Christian people not for any nostalgic attachment to it for its own sake, but always for the *real thing* which it represents and conveys: the thing which is catholic, essential, lasting.

TOO NEAT FOR GOD   September 19

While clarity of words wedded to clarity of mind can be used by God's servants to grasp and expound his truth, the same clarity can also distort and deceive by being more neat than God can ever be. (CP)

THE PERILS OF HUMAN EXPRESSION   September 20

When God makes himself known to the prophet Amos, the prophet says, "He showed me a basket of summer fruit". The divine word here uses a phenomenon of nature as its medium. So when

179

Jesus reveals the character of God in his teaching he tells a story, or describes a similitude, or creates an image intelligible to his hearers from within their experience.

Yet, in the knowledge of God, there is a beyondness; for no image, no parable, no dogmatic definition, no words, suffice to convey God's reality. "We are compelled to attempt what is unattainable", wrote St. Hilary of Poitiers, "to climb where we cannot reach, to speak what we cannot utter. Instead of the bare adoration of faith, we are compelled to entrust the deep things of religion to the perils of human expression".

The beyondness in the knowledge of God is realised in the silence of adoration, and in the phase of mystical experience which is beyond words and images. (SS)

BE GENTLE WITH OTHERS   September 21

In using historical imagery about God—imagery which is likely always to be with us—be very tender towards the simple, unquestioning piety of those who picture, believe, pray, and ask no questions.

But with that tenderness combine a readiness to be often asking—gently of others and severely of oneself—"What are we really saying?", and "What do we really mean?" It is in such asking and answering that faith becomes lively. (CPT)

FROM ALONGSIDE   September 22

There is a kind of *kenosis* or self-emptying in the Christian's witness and influence in society. Christians span both worlds, and their possession of the new world should enhance their power to talk to the old world—not as from a pedestal of the converted, but as from alongside.

Let me give a practical illustration. Suppose a trade union is bullying a man and sending him to Coventry because he refuses to toe the line. A Christian in the trade union protests. What is the nature of his protest, and how can it be effective? He will not say, "You heathen fellows know nothing of justice and liberty; we converts know better, and have justice and liberty in our converted society". No, that is the kind of hot-gospelling which disallows the moral validity of the natural order. The Christian protests against the bullying by a trade union in the name of the justice and liberty which lie at the root of *human* association as made by God, and at the root of trade unionism itself. That is the true form of Christian protest. The *ad hominem* approach is not only good tactics, but the soundest doctrine.

The courage and humility with which the protest is made, with a power to prick the heart—these come indeed from a supernatural source, from a life hid with Christ in God. But just because the source of the courage and the humility are supernatural, and from Christ, the witness has the "*kenotic*" power of coming down to the natural, and appealing to the natural in the terms of the natural. (DEA).

PINNED TO A GLOBE   September 23

Now if we lived floating in space, it might seem that it would be easier for us to love God, and to serve him without so many distractions. But we live pinned to a globe of earth by a law of gravity. and with that earth we are very much involved.

We need to eat, drink, marry, beget children, live in communities and organise ourselves, and organise the forces of the earth for these complex purposes.

It is in this complexity of a common life, and a relation to nature, that we are set to glorify God. In the eighth psalm we find the classical expression of this. Man is described as possessing a sovereignty over the created world which he is to exercise as one who is himself under God's sovereignty. That is the picture of what is meant to be: man controlling the world's products and processes in dependence on God, giving glory to him, and living in a community of mutual love and service, neither exploiting nature selfishly nor aggrandising himself, but using all as God's creature and servant.

But there was a crash. The Bible has a story about it. You may recall the picture:

> And they heard the voice of the Lord walking in the garden in the cool of the day: and the man and his wife hid themselves among the trees of the garden. And the Lord God called unto the man and said unto him, Where art thou?

It is the story of the disobedience of Adam and Eve. There is no necessity for a Christian to believe it to be history: indeed, there are reasons why it cannot be literal history. But the story is superb, and true in what it says in parable or poetry, devastatingly true: that the human race has upset its right relation to the Creator by forming the habit of pride, self-aggrandisement, false independence. The story, with the divine voice calling to disobedient man, "Where art thou?" tells of humanity as a whole, and tells of you in particular. In part you are subject to the traditions and influences of the human race which has collectively gone wrong. In part, you yourself are guilty of acts of pride, exalting yourself into the place of your Creator. (ICF)

A STORY OF BOILS   September 24

There are three outstanding moral issues on a world scale which we have to face. One is the urgency of radical disarmament in all forms of weapons, so that no nation possesses enough forces to be able to start an aggressive war. Another is the need of a radical change in the attitude of races, white and black, towards one another. The third is the need for countries which are rich and prosperous to give of their resources to help those in terrible poverty. It is outrageous that some countries enjoy a high standard of living while others experience acute poverty and hunger.

Let me tell a story which shows all this in perspective. There was once a man who had three nasty big boils, and he went to the doctor and asked for each of them to be treated or removed. And the doctor said, "My dear fellow, I can do nothing permanent with those boils unless we get rid of the poison in your system which is causing them". So, too, the human race, very sick and having at least three terrible boils in the social and moral order, wants to be rid of them because it would be happier without them. But this human race does not grasp that the trouble is a poison in the system, and that the sickness is that of a deep derangement in the relation of mankind to the Creator. And some of the worst boils are ones which the patient has not yet noticed to be there.

Go to the root. "Do justly, love mercy, walk humbly with thy God", said the prophet. Far and wide, men and women try fitfully to do the first and the second, and the third is pushed aside. So justice is blind, and mercy too often calculating and patronising. The root is the right relation of man to the Creator: and when Christians are concerned about what they call worship, they are concerned not with something remote or escapist, but with the root of the world's predicament.

It is God alone who comes to put us right. "He taketh up the simple out of the dust, and lifteth the poor out of the mire." (ICF)

KALEIDOSCOPE September 25

The Church is sent to declare the Gospel to the world. The Church's mission has been an exciting story. It is not a story of smooth and steady expansion, as if first this country became securely Christian, and then the next, and the next, until the globe was covered. No, the story is a kaleidoscope one of ups and downs, of scandal and glory, of set-backs and advances.

We see the Christian faith coming to Britain, and meanwhile

Jerusalem—the Gospel's original base—has passed into Muslim hands. The last century saw the wonderful spread of the Christian faith in Asia and Africa—a stupendous missionary century. Then, godless systems invaded ancient homes of Christian civilisation: Russia, Germany.

And what of the decay in our own country? Civilisations which were once fairly Christian can become stale and complacent, affluent, and insensitive to the needs of humanity.

It is among those ups and downs of divine judgments and divine victories that God's reign comes. Perhaps we in England may one day learn the Christian faith again from Christians of Asia or Africa. If so, I should love to think of a black Archbishop of York holding a mission to the University of Oxford, and telling a future generation of the scandal and the glory of the Church. (ICF)

From an address at Oxford University while Archbishop of York

SEETHING UNREST   September 26

Notice the new role which the race problem is assuming in many parts of the world.

To my generation, with its old-fashioned liberalism, the race problem meant getting white people and black people to be kind to one another. To the younger generation, the race problem often means the seething unrest of black people who will tolerate white domination no longer, and who ask why—if it was right for us white people in Europe to fight for liberation from Hitler—it is wrong for them to fight for liberation from their oppressors. (CPT)

THE AUTHORITY OF CAESAR   September 27

What were the obligations of citizens—in Germany and in other countries—under the Hitler Fascist regime? I would say it was right for them to obey authority in matters like following the rule of the road—those sorts of instant kinds of orderliness that the State can regulate. But when it comes to the matter of the State setting about exterminating the Jews, then it was behaving in such a way as to become apostate from its proper function as an authority under God.

So long as the Roman state was a just state exercising order, it was right for Christians to be obedient, however much they disliked it. But when the state started deifying itself by empire worship—a form of idolatry—it began to destroy its own divine function.

CONTRADICTION September 28

If it is wrong to bless a guerrilla movement, it is no less wrong tacitly to uphold a regime which uses violence towards its population. (CP)

CHRISTIAN ANALYSIS September 29

Christian conviction gives the true analysis of what is wrong with any political or economic system, such as Communism.

An evil system is one which so treats human beings as to contradict the worth they have as persons possessing everlasting value in the eyes of God.

THE WASHING OF THE WORLD September 30

God wants to wash away quarrels and hatred and war. God wants to wash away all violence and cruelty. God wants to wash away all sexual immorality and undermining of family life. God wants to wash away the evils of drug taking. God wants to wash away racial discrimination. God wants to wash away all injustice towards individuals, so that the world will be really clean.

But we who are Christian people must not only say that the world must be washed; we must also say that we ourselves must be washed. And that means that again and again we must be ready to confess our sins, and to ask Christ to forgive us.

And when Christ forgives us, it is like when he washed the feet of the apostles in the upper room. The Christians of the future must be less proud and more humble. They will not only denounce the sins of the world, they will have their own sins put right by Christ's absolution.

OCTOBER

THE WRONG DIVIDING LINE October 1

We need to remind ourselves that the New Testament, while it bids us hope firmly and hope joyfully, nowhere encourages us to expect that the coming of the kingdom of God will happen in a steady progression. It was characteristic of much theology in the last century and the early years of the present century to think of the kingdom of God in that way. Mankind would become gradually more religious, more ethical in its behaviour, more educated, more just in its social and economic life, and so through the steady growth of religion and knowledge the Kingdom of God would come.

But neither our Lord nor the apostles encourage such an idea. Rather do parts of their teaching suggest that there may be a series of catastrophic happenings in which evil shows itself with new power and perhaps there will be a final manifestation of evil in horrible forms, before Christ finally triumphs. To say this is not to lessen the confidence of the Christian hope. It is only to insist that it is always hope in the God of Calvary and Easter.

Nor does the New Testament encourage us to suppose that if only the church were really Christlike and really efficient in doing its work, then people everywhere would be readily converted. The "if only" idea can be very misleading. We dare not overlook the words

187

of St. Paul: "If our gospel is veiled it is veiled to those who are perishing. In their case the God of this world has blinded the minds of the unbelieving to keep them from seeing the light of the gospel of the glory of God in the face of Jesus Christ" (2 Cor. 4. 3–6).

The simplicity of the gospel does not mean that it can be easily grasped by those who are worldly and impenitent. It means that it poses the issue in a sharp and simple way and, in so doing, divides mankind. At present the church is not Christlike enough, the division is often at the wrong line: there are some inside the Church who would be outside the Church if the Church were more Christlike, and there are some outside the Church who would be drawn inside if it were a more Christlike Church. If the Church bore its witness more faithfully, certain issues would be seen more sharply and simply. (FCC)

NOT ON THE WORLD'S TERMS   October 2

Good works are the urgent outcome of faith, and the lack of them may often be an occasion for divine judgment on the Church. There can be no true faith which does not overflow in actions of compassion and human reconciliation. But woe to the Church if it thinks it can justify itself to the world, and find its own security, in a successful programme of philanthropy. It was such a justification of his own mission which our Lord decisively rejected as he moved towards the Cross for which he had been sent for the world's redemption.

The Church is called to serve without ceasing; but never to commend itself to the world by providing what the world would most like and approve on the world's own terms. When the Church tries to commend itself in this way it can do good, it can win admiration for a while, but it can lose the power to lead men to repentance, to divine forgiveness, and to the God of the Resurrection. (FCC)

The unity for which our Lord prayed embraces aspects of human life more numerous than those which belong to the limited realm of ecclesiastical concerns. Through the unity of the *ecclesia* all people and all things are destined to become one in Christ.

There are today, not least among the younger people in the Church and on the fringe of the Church, many who are wearied by ecumenism because it often seems to be a movement enjoyed by ecclesiastics preoccupied with ecclesiastical problems. Let it be made clear that ecumenism includes every part of the healing of the wounds of races and nations. It is idle for, let us say, an Episcopal Church and a Presbyterian Church to be planning union together if in either or in both of them there is the separation of race or colour within the household of Christ.

Every breaking down of barriers which divide humanity—social, racial, economic, cultural—is part of the ecumenical task. The ecclesiastical aspects of ecumenism must be seen in this larger context. When they are so seen it is apparent that ecumenism is no hobby for church-minded people; it is a task of divine and human reconciliation in which every Christian man, woman, and child can have a share. (FCC)

To be a Christian is to be very closely united to Christ as living Lord, not alone, but in the fellowship of the Church. It means an existence in which our self-centredness is constantly challenged and defeated. The more Christ becomes your true centre, the less can your own selfish pride be the centre. The more you are drawn into the fellowship of those who belong to Christ, the less are you entangled in your selfish pride.

That is why again and again the Christian life has been called a "death to self"; it is the growth in us of Christ's own self-giving unto death. The sacraments depict this: *Baptism* was from the beginning the means whereby the convert *died* to the old life whose centre was the self, having been buried symbolically beneath the water, he stepped out into a new life whose centre was Christ in the midst of the Church's fellowship. *Holy Communion* deepens our unity with Christ who, through the media of bread and wine, feeds us with himself. But it is always his self as given to death. It is his broken body, his blood poured and offered.

These are the great realities upon which Christian people have laid hold. Some have grasped them once, and forgotten them. Some have grasped them only in a conventional and unreal way. Some have grasped them, and courageously try to be true to them among much conflict with the reassertions of self and pride. Some have grasped them, and have shown it in lives in which, notwithstanding some humiliating failures, Christ really has been apparent.

It all happens through Calvary judging us, Calvary bringing forgiveness to us, and Calvary defeating the pride which rules us. (ICF)

THE COSTLINESS OF FORGIVENESS   October 5

Do you see what a costly thing forgiveness is? Sin is an affair between you and God, your Father and Creator. It means being ungrateful to him, despising his perfect will for you, putting your pride in place of it, spitting in his face.

Similarly, when we do wrong to other people, man against man, group against group, race against race, we trample upon God's creatures. Or—here is another picture—God as Creator is like the architect of a glorious building of priceless sculpture. You choose to deface the sculpture, and hack it about.

It is thus that conscience has seen in sin a sort of dislocation of the moral order of the world. It is thus, too, that conscience has felt that nothing we can do can restore that order.

Could my zeal no respite know,
Could my tears for ever flow,
All for sin could not atone.

God is loving: he is also righteous and holy: implacably hostile
to evil. How then does forgiveness come? It cannot come as a sort
of condoning of evil, as if to say, "Never mind: it does not matter
all that much: we will make a new start, and act as if it had not
happened". Our conscience could not accept *that* procedure: indeed, the forgiveness of man by man in our experience costs more
than that.

No, forgiveness comes as an act in which God blends in one the
utter condemnation of our wrongdoing and his love for us, and
brings home to our conscience both the condemnation and the love.

We see in the crucifixion of Jesus the measure of our wrongdoing, the divine condemnation of it, and the divine love coming
to us right in the middle of the condemnation. (ICF)

SPIRITUALITY   October 6

Spirituality is a very wide term indeed. There is a spirituality
which is Christian, and a spirituality which is connected with other
religions, and there can be a sort of spirituality connected with no
religion.

I think the popularity of non-Christian forms of spirituality,
which is growing a bit in this country, is due to the failure of our
Christian Church to emphasise spirituality, prayer, and contemplation sufficiently because of the intense concentration on activism
in modern Christianity—which hasn't been a wholly good thing.

Christian activism is the expression of the second great Commandment (thou shalt love thy neighbour as thyself); but this
modern spirituality is in one way or another a recovery of the importance of the first great Commandment: man finding a relationship to eternal reality for its own sake.

Reply to a question at the London School of Economics, 1971

Christian spirituality means the relation of a man or woman to the Holy Spirit of God, the Spirit bestowed by Jesus Christ after his death, resurrection, and ascension.

It is the mission of the Holy Spirit to indwell the Christian, influencing his entire life, and when a Christian is called a spiritual person, it does not mean that his own spirit matters more than his body, but that his whole being—body, soul, and spirit—is responding to the gracious rule of the Divine Spirit within. (CEA)

TO THE FUTURE   October 8

What as Christians do we say about our duty to posterity? Is it right for a few generations of our race to use the world in ways which suit us, without the most careful and anxious thought for generations in the future?

Here we find the old doctrine of the worth of every man and woman in God's creation through the ages crying out aloud. This doctrine may stretch our imaginations far into the future, and make us ask whether it is for us to plan prosperity for ourselves, and to enjoy such affluence as we can, without thought and action for the benefit of those persons whose lives will be in God's far distant future. (FFF)

THE WITNESS OF THE CINQUE PORTS   October 9

The stretch of coastline covered by the Cinque Ports (along the coastline of Sussex and Kent) has known invasions which happened, and invasions which mercifully did not. The Romans came. Hengist and Horsa came. And just on nine centuries ago, William of Normandy came. Who could now regret any of those comings? They served to make our nation—with its blending of diverse elements, with its strange unity of character, with its independence, and with its many links with Europe.

In this history we can trace the good hand of a divine providence, securing liberties, inspiring ideals, creating opportunities, and bringing judgment upon ourselves. This is our God for ever and ever.

We thank him for his goodness and loving-kindness through the centuries. We pray that, at a time when so many neglect him, disbelieve him, or are apathetic to his moral laws, he will raise up his power and come among us, and with great might succour us. May he bring men and women and children to know him and love him. May he bring reconciliation and peace to the nations and races. May he give us all of what we need so greatly at this time in our country; the will to make sacrifices for the common good. May he invade human hearts everywhere, and conquer them by his love. This God is our God for ever and ever.

On the occasion of the appointment of the new Warden of
the Cinque Ports, 1966

EUROPEAN ATTITUDES   October 10

It was never likely that the Christian ideal of a Europe serving the world would easily come to dominate European attitudes and policies. It is true that statesmen are ready to talk about the service that Europe can give to the world. But when anxiety about our people's own standard of living and economic burdens looms large —as it does just now—even the talk of our duty to the Third World easily disappears.

No, if the Christian ideal for Europe is to prevail, there must be the continuous pressure of those who believe in that ideal, moulding opinions, attitudes, policies. It means that certain central Christian doctrines must deeply influence the European attitude.

There is the doctrine that power is properly linked with service: "The rulers of the nations lord it over them and are called benefactors, but it shall not be so with you". There is the doctrine that on this small planet we are all members one of another. There is the doctrine that to serve the man or woman who is hungry is to serve Christ himself.

It is by remembering these truths, and putting them into practice, that we see the difference between a Europe and a Christian Europe. (CP)

CONSECRATING EVERYDAY LIFE   October 11

I speak of liturgy as a fact in Christendom which has appeared in a variety of forms and phases, with different spiritual emphasis.

In the Latin rite there is a vivid sense of the Cross, where sinful men and women look upon him whom their sins have pierced, and know that in Jesus crucified is salvation, though the thought of the heavenly tabernacle is never far away. In the liturgies of the Orthodox East, both Greek and Slavonic, the joy of the Resurrection is prominent, and the worshippers know themselves to be already in the heavenly places with Christ. In the case of the Anglican liturgy it is necessary, for a right understanding, to see not only the rite in England, but also the rites in the United States (derived from Scotland), in Canada, in the West Indies, in India, and in various parts of Africa, giving as they do a picture of the growing liturgical life mindful alike of the one sacrifice of Calvary, and of the heavenly priesthood of our Lord.

Today, liturgical movements in many parts of Christendom put a renewed emphasis upon the participation of the faithful in the liturgy, and upon the down-to-earth aspect of the liturgy as the means of consecrating the common, everyday life of the people to God. In this way the liturgy is seen to belong alike to the involvement and to the detachment in the mission of the Church. (CEA)

AN ACT FULL OF AWE   October 12

There is a tendency to emphasise that Holy Communion is "corporate". We are urged to speak of "our communion", and to suspect the phrase "my communion". Certainly a truth has been recovered here. But Holy Communion involves, none the less, the responsible act of an individual, and it is an act full of awe and dread. If Holy Communion unites a man with his fellows, it does at the same time set him alone with his Lord, as at the hour of death and the day of judgment.

> Just as I am, without one plea,
> But that thy blood was shed for me,
> And that thou bidst me come to thee,
> O Lamb of God, I come.

The awe in the individual's approach to Holy Communion, which characterised both the Tractarians and the Evangelicals of old, stands in contrast to the ease with which our congregations come tripping to the altar week by week.

I remember talking not long ago to an old man, utterly sincere, who did not feel he could come to Holy Communion because he simply dared not approach so great a thing. Of course there was an answer to him. But I could not help thinking that the man's words represented something which has an honourable place in Christian history.

I suggest that we should read and ponder the long Exhortation in the Communion service in the Prayer Book, which brings home how the reception of the Communion is dreadful as well as precious, and reminds us of the need for confession of sin, and the possibility of the "benefit of absolution". We of the clergy are sent not to bring people to be "communicants", so much as to bring them (and ourselves) into union with our Lord by the careful use of Communion, prayer, and penitence. (DEA)

THE NORM OF WORSHIP October 13

The Eucharist is the centre and norm of all worship. There the Divine Word is revealed in the lections and propers for the nourishment of our souls. But at the climax of the rite, through the consecration prayer, the whole mystery of Christ as priest, victim, and victor, is present.

In the eucharistic canon, gift and response find fullness of expression, and both are inseparable from Christ himself. The divine gift to us is Christ, and so, too, the response from man is Christ, himself our sacrifice. Our own response is made only as we are ourselves "in Christ". In the words of an Anglican eucharistic hymn, we say

> Look, Father, look on his anointed face,
> And only look on us as found in him. (CEA)

ADORATION AND OBEDIENCE   October 14

The author and agent in the Eucharist is the Word of God. The Word is proclaimed in the scripture readings, and in the preaching. Then the same Word, who is Jesus, blesses the loaf and the cup, and invites and commands us.

If we respond, and receive on our knees, nothing is more fitting to the awe and reverence of adoration. But if we respond, and receive standing—as was probably the ancient custom—nothing is more fitting as the sign of obedience: ready to go, and to save. (CP)

PEOPLE AND PRIEST   October 15

The liturgy indeed belongs to all the people. We, being many, are the one bread, one body. We take, we break, we offer, we receive, and the more vivid realisation of this has been one of the exciting marks of liturgical renewal in our time.

Where then, and why then, the priest? As celebrant he is more than the people's representative. In taking, breaking, and consecrating, he acts in Christ's name; and in the name not only of the particular congregation, but also of the Holy Catholic Church down the ages. By his office as celebrant, he symbolises the focusing of the Eucharist in the givenness of the historical gospel, and in the continuing life of the Church as rooted in the gospel. (CPT)

IN THE FACE OF SUFFERING   October 16

Living through dying is what faith means; it is what baptism means, it is what Holy Communion means; it defines the life to which every Christian is called.

For the early Christians it quite often meant martyrdom, and martyrdom is always one of the norms of the Christian vocation. But whether in martyrdom or in other ways, the Christian is called to a life of dying to self, a life in which the centre is not the self, but God and other people.

That can indeed be joyful, with the joy of forgetting self in the service of God and humanity. But in so far as pride lingers in us, the struggle with self will be painful, causing us sometimes to weep over our selfish folly. Yet, as the self is dethroned, the joy is real, and the life of those who die to self is described by Jesus as happy, joyful, blessed.

It is in this context that the Christian faces suffering. While his Christian faith may heighten rather than diminish his sensitivity to it, he will draw from his faith something of a clue to follow. He will, in the following of Christ, devote himself to the removing of suffering from his fellows wherever possible, supporting every effort to reduce its causes and its incidence.

But he will also recall the saying that, while Christ strove to remove suffering from others as if nothing could be made of it, when it came to himself he accepted it as if everything could be made of it. The Christian will be encouraged in this by the example of many men and women who have suffered in body and mind, and through their nearness to Christ have shown a sympathy, a courage, a love, a patience, and indeed a joy, which seem to come from another world. Indeed, the "glory that shall be revealed" not only belongs to the bliss of heaven to which the apostle points as beyond "the sufferings of this present time"; it also presses insistently upon the present world scene. (FFF)

THORN IN THE FLESH   October 17

St. Paul tells of a painful and perhaps disfiguring ailment which gave him great distress. He called it diabolical—a "messenger of Satan". He prayed three times for its removal. But the answer was not that, as it was contrary to the will of God, faith could remove it; nor that faith would be disillusioned if it could not. The answer was, "My grace is sufficient for thee", and for St. Paul the power of God was made "perfect in weakness".

We are to trust God's love and power. Sometimes the trust itself may be a great help towards recovery. Sometimes the trust may be some shield against sickness, where fear and worry play their dangerous parts. But the trust remains when the prayer is not answered in the way we hoped, and because it remains it enables God—where he has not healed—to make all the difference to the state of suffering.

ST. LUKE'S DAY — THE BELOVED PHYSICIAN   October 18

As the doctor sets about his task he uses his scientific knowledge and skill. But he uses it not as one who draws upon a textbook, but as one who uses imagination in applying the general to the particular, and intuition in judging whether this or that action will in this case be the more helpful. This means that his craft consists not in his science alone, but in his science together with his personality, his perseverance, sympathy, sensitivity, and understanding of persons.

I recall the ancient words of the Hippocratic oath:

I will follow that system of rule which, according to my ability and judgment, I consider for the benefit of patients, and abstain from whatever is deleterious or mischievous. I will give no deadly medicine to anyone if asked, nor suggest any such counsel; nor will I aid a woman to produce abortion. With purity and holiness I will pass my life and practise my art.

If those words have an archaic sound, they none the less describe an aspect of the doctor's craft which in our modern world is more— rather than less—indispensable.

. . . The goal of medicine is one that belongs to the Creator's design. It is his will, purpose, and delight. Suffice it only to say that Christians see in Jesus Christ the revelation of God, and the healing of the sick had a notable place in the energies of his life as the Gospels record it.

This, and the next three passages, are from an address to the
British Medical Association, 1963

FASCINATION WITH A SELF   October 19

While today many of our studies become more and more special-ised, it is more and more apparent that specialisation can obscure truth. If you are dealing with a man's health of body you do not ignore his mind, his anxieties, his fears, his frustrations, and you are involved, not with a case, but with a person; not with a body, but with a self.

Here the fascination begins, because man is so mysterious. A series of sciences explores different aspects of him, but something in man seems to elude them all: something which caused the Greek poet to say of old, "Many things are marvellous, but nothing more marvellous than man", and, earlier still, caused the psalmist to say, "I am fearfully and wonderfully made". So, just as it is hard to limit the description of the skills which a doctor uses, so it is hard to limit within the formula "health of the body" the effects and the good of his efforts.

It is considerations such as these which lead to the plea that doctors and priests should co-operate and understand one another, for when we talk of the body we involve ourselves quickly with all the aspects of a person, and when we talk of the spiritual life, we are talking of something inseparable from the bodily state.

SUCCESSES   October 20

When the doctor recalls the people he has known as patients, I suppose he may think of some as his successes—those whose health was restored against odds and obstacles—in contrast with others where disease or injury proved insuperable, and success was not attained.

Yet I believe that, as time passes and the doctor looks back upon the patients he has known, some of those he will remember most vividly, and with deep respect and reverence, will be men and women who were not "successes" in medicine or health, for the cure did not come easily, or perhaps never came at all. And yet there was something in them never to be forgotten: patience, sympathy, sensitivity, unworldliness: in a word—*saintliness*.

This saintliness goes with the power of so using suffering—when it cannot be removed—that it becomes creative in the wonderful things of character. Such people show a kind of dimension in the life of the world which does not fit our ideas of success, or health, or progress.

MAKING WHOLE   October 21

Consider the life of Christ. "He went about doing good." Healing the bodies and minds of men and women filled a large part of the record of his life. Yet the same record shows that often he restrained his activity as a healer; he refused to advertise his cures, for it was his mission to show that, while health matters greatly, there is something that matters more.

The healthy body and mind are not ends in themselves, but parts of a Kingdom of God wherein body and mind are used in the service of God and of humanity. And Christ's own final service of humanity was his ignominious death on the Cross at Calvary: an act in which suffering was filled with sacrifice, love, victory, glory. Beyond the death on Calvary there came Resurrection, eternal life, where the destiny of man—fearfully and wonderfully made—will be.

I am aware that this raises difficult questions, and with some of them the man of faith goes on wrestling. But what this thesis of Christian faith offers is a certainty of our origin—God our Creator— and a certainty of our goal—humanity totally answering God's good purpose. And between the origin and the goal, the doctor and priest work with much perplexity and darkness around them, yet with enough light to walk and work.

For both it is a divine work—to cure the sins of man: a work done with all the more eagerness when we know that man is far more wonderful than either of those crafts can describe, and that the work touches but a fragment of man's meaning and destiny. But it makes all the difference if that meaning and destiny come often into our thoughts, and they do so in the phrase, "the measure of the stature of the fullness of Christ".

THE FEET-WASHING   October 22

Jesus is with the disciples at supper on the night before the Crucifixion. The disciples have had a quarrel about the stupid question as to which of them is the greatest. The answer of Jesus is to take upon himself the role of a servant or slave, and with a basin of water and a towel he goes round the table, stooping before each disciple, and washing his feet. His answer to their pride is to show them in act the dignity of the humble service of others.

That is a theme which centuries have made familiar to us. The human race has not yet learned the lesson. Self-assertion is still written large across it. But the example given by Christ in the washing of the feet of the disciples has inspired many in every age. Many indeed who are not Christians have practised the humble service of their fellows. But the practice of it is always the test of the true Christian.

But in this scene there are other great disclosures of truth that we must not miss. Notice the opening words in which the writer introduces the story. "Jesus, knowing that the Father had given all things into his hands, and that he comes from God, and goes to God again, rises from supper, and he took a towel and girded himself." What Jesus does, he does in the awareness that divine majesty and power belong to him. He is showing to the disciples— and to us—what divine majesty is like. It is like—Jesus washing the feet of his disciples. "He that hath seen me hath seen the Father." God, the Creator and the sovereign ruler of the universe, shows his glory in humbling himself towards the created world. His humble glory is seen in the Incarnation, in the Crucifixion, in the feet-washing, in the gentle patience of all his approach to us. The scene summons us to humble ourselves before the humble God.

TEST OF HUMILITY   October 23

When Jesus, going the round of the disciples to cleanse them, comes to Simon Peter, Simon Peter vehemently objects. "Thou shalt never wash my feet." Never, never! It is easy to understand Peter's feelings. He had been learning to serve Christ, and was long-ing to serve Christ to the last. The thought of Christ serving him— it was intolerable. Never, never!

How is it with you? The most familiar test of humility is the readiness to serve others: the man who won't "come off it" and serve others labels himself as proud and bumptious. But isn't it often a very piercing test of your humility to be ready to receive another person's service? "Thank you, I can do this myself. I don't need help, and certainly not *your* help."

So it is between us and God. If we believe in him at all, we are busy serving him, and busy with our work in the world—a lot of which is probably the service of other people. But God longs for us to pause, and to let *him* serve *us*. And the service he would render to us is to come and wash from us all that he hates to see.

Do you let God serve you? If you resist the idea, or neglect it, you are being like Peter: "Thou shalt never wash my feet". But when your pride breaks, and you long for God to serve you by washing you, then, like Peter, you cry, "Lord, not my feet only, but my hands and my head".

Your service of others is more likely to go to the roots of their need if you have let God go to the roots of your need in serving you. (ICF)

THE CLAIMS OF JESUS   October 24

The theme of the teaching of Jesus is not himself and his own claims. That is striking. His theme is the kingdom, or the reign, of God. God is coming to reign. God's reign is at the door. That is his message. It is to be seen in the works which Jesus does, in the righteousness which Jesus teaches. But Jesus does not preach primarily about himself: he effaces himself in the thought and the service of the reign of God.

It is in the middle of this self-effacement that the claims of Jesus, which peep through so unobtrusively, are so overwhelming in their impact. He implies that his own place in the reign of God is such that men's relation to that reign includes their relation to Jesus himself.

Here are a few instances; you will find plenty of others. Thus: men must be ready to lose their lives so as to find them, lose their lives *"for my sake"*. What a claim! Thus again: men will one day be judged in a divine judgment, and in that judgment they will face—*Jesus*, and *he* will say to them, "I never knew you, depart from me . . ." What a claim! Thus again: there will be a new covenant, a bond between God and the people, definitive for the reign of God and its coming—and it will be "*a covenant n my blood*". What a claim!

Beneath these claims there lies a secret which peeps out now and then: Jesus is God's Son in a unique way: "No one knoweth the Father save the Son, and he to whom the Son will reveal him". What a claim! But, above all, there is this. Jesus teaches that all men must repent: they must confess their sins, and pray for God's forgiveness. But in Jesus there is no trace of repentance, no acknowledgement of sin; not for him the prayer, "Forgive us our sins".

The greatest saints have been most conscious of their sins. Not so Jesus. Without arrogance, without self-consciousness, he is not one to repent, for he is himself the source of divine righteousness to those who come to him, the medium of God's reign. Indeed, where others have died for country, for friends, for causes, for God, Jesus will die in order to lead humanity to be freed from sin, and to die to selfishness. What a claim! Consider, consider what claims these are.

Are these claims of Jesus true? If they are not, then the making of them involves either fraud on his part, or a terrible self-deception. Perhaps you are trying the line that you welcome Christ's moral teaching and admire it, but reject his own claims. It seems to me a most unconvincing line. The moral teaching and the claims are woven in one, for both concern the reign of God.

I see no escape from the dilemma: either Jesus is fraudulent, or his claim is true: either we judge him for being terribly amiss, or we let him judge us. That was, in fact, the dilemma that cut through the consciences of his contemporaries. (ICF)

"I AM THE LIGHT"   October 25

Jesus said, "I am the light". One of the oldest hymns used by Christians—St. Paul quotes it—was "Sleeper awake: rise from the dead: Christ shall give you light".

Jesus enables you to see. By your allegiance to him you begin to see God by faith. You begin to see yourself with your illusions about yourself shaken, and your pride shattered. You begin to see other people as they really are, through eyes like those of Jesus, and not through the eyes of your distorted prejudices.

You also see the world and its needs with new awareness, and know that to serve others in their suffering is to serve Jesus himself. (ICF)

"THY KINGDOM COME"   October 26

What is our hope concerning this world in which we are now living? Certainly Christ encourages us to have hope concerning it. We are to pray, "Thy kingdom come on earth", and so to hope that God's rule may become apparent in the world everywhere.

Thus we hope to see races free from injustice to one another, for racial strife is a denial of the divine image in man. We hope to see nations so using the earth's resources and economic structures that all may have enough to eat, instead of some being affluent while others starve. We hope to see war, and the possibility of war, banished. We hope to see family life everywhere secure and stable, happy and unselfish, with sex fulfilling its true use in lifelong marriage. We hope to see chastity, honesty, and compassion prevail. We hope to see these things happen as part of a deep reconciliation between man and God through Jesus Christ. We hope to see people brought everywhere into fellowship with God through him.

In all this we hold in one our hope about earth and our hope about heaven. A Christian can scarcely separate these hopes, as Jesus is the Lord of both earth and heaven. (FFF)

THE COMING   October 27

We need to warn ourselves against a false view of how the kingdom of God comes in the world.

In the latter part of the last century, and in the early years of this, it was often supposed by Christians in the West that by a kind of steady progression the world would become more Christian in belief, more civilised in behaviour, more mature in scientific achievements, more happy, and more prosperous, all these forces moving together in a steady ascent towards a kind of Utopia to be identified with the Kingdom of God. But it is impossible to find sanction in the New Testament for thinking that the Kingdom of God will come in that kind of way.

Neither our Lord nor the apostles encourage us to expect a steady advance of the good and a steady regression of the evil, still less an idea that this would go hand in hand with culture and prosperity. Rather does some of the language of the New Testament suggest an ever-identifying conflict between the evil and the good, issuing in a costly victory by the way of the Cross.

So it is that the hope of the apostolic writers is focused far less upon the coming reign of God as a state of things which can be described, than upon the coming of Christ himself. It is upon *him* that the hope is focused. *He* will come into his own. He will come to us: we shall go to him. It is in Christ, for Christ, that we hope. (FFF)

THE CONVERT											October 28

When Paul and Silas were in prison in Philippi, and there was an earthquake, and they were liberated, and the jailer was converted and—with his whole household—baptised, it was a *jailer* who was converted: not a man in a vacuum. And we would hope that as a Christian jailer he was a different person in his dealings with people and with his job. (CPT)

THE GOOD AND THE BEAUTIFUL							October 29

Looking at the long story of the evolution of the world, of the animal species, and of man, you see the emergence of the phenomena

of what you call "the good", "the beautiful", "saintly", "perfect":
values in character and behaviour which excite admiration and
imitation.

Are these phenomena haphazard products of the evolutionary
process? Are they passing incidents in nature and history, like a
thunderstorm which comes and goes, or a brontosaurus species
which had its day and became extinct? Or are they fairly to be
called supreme things for the sake of which we ourselves exist—and
perhaps the whole process which produced our race has existed?
Are self-sacrifice, unselfish love, moral integrity not mere incidents,
but the goal and the meaning of the whole? (ICF)

PEOPLE IN GLASS HOUSES   October 30

It should be clear to us that if we give exhortations to other
people about their duty we must see the corollaries for our country
as a whole, and for ourselves.

For instance, if we say (as I have often said myself in these past
weeks) that the miners ought not to strike because by striking they
are thwarting the battle against inflation, and hurting the community, including themselves, we have to remember that others in the
community have done well through property or dividends, and we
all have to ask ourselves whether we have never helped ourselves in
selfish ways. A country which was itself a model of just and equi-
table dealing would be in a stronger position to say "don't" to any
group which helped inflation.

And if we say (and I have said it myself in the past months) that
it is tiresome of the Arabs to cause difficulties about oil, we must
ask what very hungry people may think of our own economy in
relation to the Third World. Crisis forces us to see problems in a
larger context, and to realise that we are members one of another.

Most important of all, perhaps, we are compelled to see the
question of standards of living not within narrow or national limits,
but in relation to the world scene. It is being said that one of the

morals is that we have had too high standards, and ought to repent of this, and settle down to lower standards as a better way of life.

That is rather too facile, because there is nothing specially Christian in having lower standards. Neither "doing with less" nor "having it so good" is in itself Christian or un-Christian. There are those in this country for whom we must long to see a better standard of living.

No, the point is rather that the world as a whole, with its vastly increasing population, is going to be hard put to it in feeding the world's population as a whole; that the world's whole economy is in crisis; and that the western states cannot count upon the continuance of standards which they have taken for granted as the unquestioned order of the day.

We are thus going to be compelled to see our world economy in terms of our being members one of another, and, while we try to raise the standards of some whose standards are far too low, we have to be ready ourselves for a new simplicity of living.

After all, Christ assures us that such a way can be happy and blessed, and events now seem to suggest that it may be the only way of survival.

From a Presidential Address to the General Synod, February 1974

THE CHURCH AND HISTORY   October 31

Every Church is always affected both for good and for ill by the various historical situations in which it finds itself: It cannot control these situations very much, and if it tries to do so by enforcement of its own authority or by secular power it does more harm than good.

Our Lord has once and for all taught the Church that it best does his work as he did it: by long-suffering, patience, and the endurance of suffering and death.

Yet every Church, moved by a true and inevitable sense of responsibility for the Church and for its children—though not always by that motive alone—has reached out after power with which to protect its people and its possessions, and to master the course of history.

NOVEMBER

ALL SAINTS   November 1

If the god to whom we pray is God the Creator and the Saviour and the Father of Jesus, then four-fifths of our prayer to him will be enjoying his presence: enjoying him, looking towards him, being hungry and thirsty for him, just seeking him because he is good and lovable and great and wonderful and glorious.

If we ask, "How can we thus find God?" then think of the wonder of his presence and his goodness in the beauties of nature; or think of his wonder in the life of Jesus as we read and absorb the life of Jesus; or think of his goodness to us in the special blessings he has given to each of us in our lives.

At All Saints-tide, think of the wonderful presence and power of God in the lives of good and lovely people, some of whom we have known well, some not so well.

In all these ways God is intimate, near, and lovable, and evoking for us a joy in him and his presence. It is that kind of joy in him and in his presence which is the real essence of Christian prayer.

COMMUNION OF SAINTS   November 2

One consequence of the mystery of Christ is that Christian

people don't stand—so to say—on the ground of the present moment, and view past generations, or their comrades in paradise, as people some distance away from them.

No, we see the present moment more clearly and bravely because our stance is within the Communion of Saints. How closely, how lovingly, they are praying with us today.

FREEDOM   November 3

My freedom does not mean my ability to do what I like as and when I like: it means my ability to choose some goal or end, and to unify all my powers in the consistent pursuit of that goal or end.

That is a freedom for the whole person, a freedom which involves an ideal *for* which one is free; a freedom which involves restraints which a person makes for himself, but which the community can also help him make in a common pursuit of freedom. It is, above all, not only a freedom *from* this and that and the other, but a freedom *for* something greater than oneself. And in so far as it is a freedom *from*, it is a freedom from oneself, from the arbitrary tyranny which the self can impose upon itself.

JESUS, THE FREE MAN   November 4

It is the belief of Christianity that God alone is perfectly free; in him alone is freedom in its perfection. And God created the human race in his own image in order to share with human beings the freedom which is his.

Man, God's creature and child, becomes free by knowing God's will and purpose, and organising himself in the doing of it, with God's glory as his goal. Hence the great phrase of the apostle, "the glorious freedom of the sons of God"—those who are free from self-will so as to enjoy the service of God, and of one another, perfectly. Hence, too, the words of the old Christian prayer: "*cui servire regnare*", God "whom to serve is to reign", God, "whose service is perfect freedom".

Consider Jesus Christ. We who are Christians believe him to be divine. But we see him also as the man in whom freedom is supremely embodied: Jesus, the free man.

There is, in the records of his life, his freedom from tradition: he fearlessly treads new ground when he knows it is right. There is his freedom from the conventions of society: he associates with harlots and people whom society regards as beyond the pale. There is his freedom from the pressure of circumstances: though he feels keenly the troubles of the world around him with an acute sensitivity to pain and wrong and tragedy, he has a serenity, an inner peace of a wonderful kind. There is also his freedom from the domination of the ideas of his own age, or any age: he is ruled neither by old ideas, nor by the newest ideas and fashions of thought, and this gives a timeless authority to him and his teaching, as one who speaks to any or every generation.

There is in Jesus a freedom from something, and a freedom for something.

CITIZENS OF THE KINGDOM   November 5

Divine law is not abolished by Jesus, far from it. Divine law is fulfilled and deepened, and if we are faithful to Jesus we know that the divine law still has a very central place in the kingdom of God.

But the heart of the ethics of Jesus is not in law or a code of rules; it is a relationship of men and women and children to God. They are to live towards God, live with the sensitive side of their being turned towards God; and in this being near to God, in trusting him and loving him, they will find themselves reflecting his character, being possessed by his rule: and that means living as citizens of the kingdom of God.

For instance, men are to love their enemies. Why? How? Because

213

God's providential goodness is quite indiscriminate. He gives sunshine and he gives rain indiscriminately to all of us, the good and the bad alike, and if we are utterly near to God we shall just find ourselves reflecting this indiscriminate love of his, and shall love our enemies as well as our friends.

Again, one of the evils in human life is fear, and fear springing from lack of trust is the soil in which so much self-concern and protective selfishness grows. But live near to God, rejoicing in God's providential care, and you won't worry, you won't fear, you will be every hour and every minute in the presence of God who cares for the lilies and clothes the grass, and cares infinitely for you.

That habitual nearness to God and trust in his providence will remove fear from your life, and, being without fear, you will be without those horrid sins that have fear as their root.

OUR CONSTANT REWARD   November 6

God forgives all of us, however terrible our behaviour may have been, however undeserving of God's forgiveness we may be. God has forgiven us so much that, living near to God, within God's kingdom or reign, we shall find ourselves forgiving others instead of being resentful towards them, because we are just reflecting the nearness of God towards whom our lives are being lived.

Such is the righteousness of a Godward relationship which is rooted in the attitude of childlike dependence and receptivity towards God.

Now in many ways the ethical teaching of Jesus is terribly hard, and sometimes it is terribly hard because Jesus gives such stern calls to sacrifice and renunciation—though sacrifice and renunciation, in the teaching of Jesus, are joyful if they are just a part of this nearness to God, and God himself is our constant reward. But the greatest difficulty in the ethical teaching of Jesus is not nearly so much, I would say, his stern calls to renunciation as his insistence on the generosity of God's giving to us, demanding that we shall be utterly humble, utterly childlike, utterly receptive.

It is this dependence, humility, receptivity, childlikeness that is the hard thing that Jesus demands: that we shall be humble enough to receive a goodness, a righteousness, that is all God's gift and never our own achievement.

EDUCATION AND CHRISTIANITY   November 7

We should have a clear definition of our terms.

Education: by that I understand not merely the imparting of knowledge, but the drawing out of the powers of mind, spirit, and body; the evoking of a reverence for the truth, and the use of the imagination in its pursuit.

Christianity: by that I understand a distinctive belief and way of life connected with the Bible, the belief that there is one God, supreme and righteous, who created the world, and therein the human race, which is distinct from the Creator in its utter creaturely dependence upon him, yet akin to him as made "in his own image" for fellowship with him; that mankind has wilfully deviated from the divine will and brought catastrophe upon itself; that Jesus Christ came as the perfect revelation of God and as—by his death and resurrection and the gift of the Spirit—the restorer of mankind; that Jesus Christ is the living, contemporary Lord, through whom we have eternal life here already and beyond the grave. (DEA)

CHRISTIAN EDUCATION   November 8

A Christian view of education is one which bears in mind not just biblical instruction or the ecclesiastical element, but the *unity of education as a whole*.

Perhaps you teach science. Take a large view of it. What does it include? The understanding of the visible world: not only the data which the mechanistic sciences deal with, but all the data of

215

order and beauty in the world—"nature" in its older and comprehensive meaning. In your own teaching you will be touching only a fragment of this, but you can do so in such a way as to evoke not only knowledge, but also awe and wonder.

Perhaps you teach the "arts": literature or history. Then you will be teaching your pupils to see something of the greatness and littleness, the grandeur and frailty of human life, with the wonders of character and conscience.

Or perhaps your biggest interest is not in the subject, but in the child to whom you teach it, as you draw out his power of thought, memory, appreciation, and wonder—including perhaps some wonder at the meaning of his own existence.

Though I am a churchman and a theologian, I am not speaking out of propaganda for my trade, but out of respect for yours, if you will see yourself in its integrity, its wholeness. Let those who care for education see what great issues of human life it includes: let those who care for Christianity see how education, by being its true self, can be religious through and through.

I end with some words of a Christian humanist, who wrote at a time when civilisation seemed to be tottering: St. Augustine said it should be our task "to orient this earthly peace towards that heavenly peace which is peace indeed". (DEA)

FROM THE ATOM TO THE SAINT   November 9

The "conflict between religion and science", familiar to us since Victorian times, is a troublesome result of the older "split" in the unity of Christian humanism: on the one hand a bad presentation of religion, making wrong claims for the Bible: on the other hand, a narrowed conception of science which treats *all* knowledge as if it proceeded on the lines of the mechanical sciences, and forgets the complexity of "nature" in its totality from the atom to the saint.

One result of the cleavage within our tradition is the difficulty which the teacher of religion has in being intelligible to the person whose mental processes have been trained in a modern scientific curriculum. The unintelligibility is sometimes mutual.

The traditional Christian language is sometimes unintelligible not because it is archaic, but because it is poetical. I would plead with schools to teach poetry, *any* good poetry, and arouse a love for it in their pupils. This at least prepares the ground for Christian imagery to speak to those whose mental training has been far removed from it. (DEA)

SAINTLINESS   November 10

The modern world is impatient of all claims to speak with *a priori* authority, to proclaim ideas as authoritative, and to demand that they shall regulate human life.

But the authority of persons through the lives they lead is a very different matter. It would seem that the word "holy" suggests an *a priori* conception linked with religion, but perhaps the alternative word "saint", or "saintly", has a different ring, and suggests simply lives of a certain character, lives which are a part of the world's empirical experience.

I have a suspicion that where the idea of being holy cuts no ice at all, the description of human lives as "saintly" sometimes rings an authentic human bell. "He was a saint". "He was a bit of a saint." And when we ask what the character of a saint is, what do we find? Not one who excels in all the virtues, but one who may be very conscious of faults and failings, yet has in that awareness a marvellous humility which attracts and wins.

And because Godwardness is the secret of a saint, he has at once a sensitivity to the sufferings of his fellows—feeling, caring, and bearing—and a kind of heavenly serenity which brings strength to the troubled. Those who have felt his presence find something a little "other" and awe-inspiring. And they think of him as one who *is* something, rather than as one who necessarily *does* so many things for the world.

Do you remember the story of St. Martin and his vision?

One day Martin, the soldier-saint, was praying, and there appeared before him a blazing light, and within it was a radiant, joyful figure, robed like a king with a jewelled crown and gold-embroidered shoes. And his voice said, "Martin, recognise him whom you see. I am Christ. I am about to descend to the earth, and I am showing myself to you first". A moment or two later the voice went on, "Why do you hesitate, Martin, to believe me? I am Christ". And Martin replied, "The Lord Jesus did not foretell that he would come in purple and crowned with gold. I will not believe that Christ is come unless I see him in the dress and in the form in which he suffered". The apparition vanished. Martin knew it was a temptation of the devil.

There is the issue. If the Easter faith is to prevail in the world it will not be through a "triumphalist" Church, but a Church which has the marks of sacrifice. (CP)

MARTYRDOM   November 12

Not all Christians are called to actual martyrdom. But all are called to something of which martyrdom is the external sign—the sharing in the self-giving, the offering, the selflessness of the Lord. (CP)

CALLED TO BE SAINTS   November 13

The first step is the primary one of communion with God himself, the readiness to go apart in quietness, waiting upon God. "Be still and know that I am God." "God thou art my God, early will I seek thee." The next step which follows is penitence, for the authentic sense of God's presence leads quickly to that grief at the sight of ourselves beside him. Our contrition and confession of sinfulness mean that in all our busy-ness in serving God we are ready to pause, and to let him serve us in the absolving of those things in us which he hates to see.

Would that among all of us, clergy and laity alike, these needs had a larger place: the practice of retreat and withdrawal to wait upon God in stillness, and the practising of confessing our sins with care and cost. It is for the fulfilment of the Church's mission in the world that these needs are urgent.

The Church must indeed be deeply involved with the present age, studying it, learning its techniques, sensitive to its aspirations and its fears; and yet as a Church we shall grapple with the present age best if there is in our church life that otherworldly strain of which All Saints Day is the reminder. We best do God's will now if there is in us the longing for God for God's own sake which sees our present tasks in the light of our heavenly goal, where "his servants shall serve him, and they shall see his face". (CEA)

RIGHTEOUSNESS AND PROSPERITY   November 14

Crisis affects our life in all its aspects. It confronts us with the divine judgment upon our whole civilisation. It confronts us with the claims of righteousness. "Seek *me* and you shall live, says the Lord." It is not surprising that we should be in a mess in a society with so much love of money and pleasure, too little concern for our fellows who suffer, and too little concern for the sacredness of human life—as is seen, for instance, in the present role of abortion in our country. When our civilisation loses true values and true priorities, it is not surprising that the law of divine judgment is apparent.

The call to God and repentance, however, is sometimes presented in a way which can be very misleading: as when people say that if only we turned to God then there would be the foundation of a secure, stable, happy, and fairly prosperous society. That may be so. But the idea that righteousness leads to prosperity is the doctrine of the Book of Deuteronomy rather than the doctrine of our

Lord and the apostles. It was not for the purpose of guaranteeing a stable and secure society that our Lord and the apostles taught what they did. I recall the words of F. C. Burkitt: "Christianity was from the first organised for a time of catastrophe".

It is doubtful from history and experience whether countries which are righteous and God-fearing are necessarily also stable, secure, and prosperous. The answer of history has sometimes been yes, and sometimes no.

No, we summon the people to turn to God because we are in a mess, and because God is true and righteous and he will know what to do with us when we turn to him. Clearly, however, a return to God which included those human attitudes which I have tried to describe in relation to our present crisis could not fail to affect industrial and social relationships in our own country and beyond it, and to open our eyes to a more Christian society.

From a Presidential Address to the General Synod, 1974

THE FALL   November 15

There is no need to suppose that primitive mankind was perfect. The "fall", as Christians call the disaster, need not have been a crash from primitive perfection; think of it as a deviation of progress right away from the path of man's right response to the promptings of God.

Again, there is no need to suppose that this belief is incompatible with evolution. There has, indeed, been not only the emergence of our race from animal ancestry, but also the genuine moral and spiritual progress of our race.

It is in the middle of this progress that man's calamitous state has shown itself. Civilisations have come with their vast achievements in culture and morality, yet they have crashed, for at the height of their achievement there was not the humble sensitivity of creature to Creator. So too with the individual: your own virtues can grow and be very real, and then it turns out that these very virtues are aiding and abetting the hard core of pride which is deep within you.

So it is with those who are virtuous and moral: it is otherwise with that exciting person, the saint; for the saint is humble before God. (ICF)

TALKING IN A VACUUM   November 16

How great here is the contrast between the environment of the Gospel in the Graeco-Roman world, and its environment in secular society today. Then there was indeed a gulf between Christianity and paganism, and it was by a miracle of conversion that a man became Christian. But there was no lack of community of discourse between Christian and pagan. There were Stoicism and Platonism, the mystery-religions and the Hermetic writings—a world ready to discuss deity, conscience, salvation, and the fear of death. The Christian and pagan could be talking about the same sort of things and using the same sort of words: the Gospel of St. John is a signal illustration of this process. Today, how different things are! Where is a community of discourse to be found between the Christian faith and minds moulded by contemporary secularism?

It is here that theology today has its stupendously difficult task. The secularist world has no congenial philosophies with which theology can make alliance, but it contains many *gropings*. We need, with sympathy and sensitivity and the spirit of learners, to put ourselves alongside these gropings, to be ready for Christ's sake to grope with those who grope. And if we do so, we may discover in unexpected places "altars to the unknown God", even though the word God is not used. Here, I believe, are some of theology's exciting, though as yet undefinable, tasks.

PRESENTING THE FAITH   November 17

The Bible's own method, and especially Christ's own method, is seen again and again to be the method of parable. It uses the daily circumstances of life in city, town, or village, in home or in workshop, as illustrations of the relations of God and man, and challenges minds and consciences within the area of their own experience.

But this must be supplemented by dialogue which starts where people are, evokes from them what are the things which for them are absolute or imperative, and discovers how these things—however non-religious in their language—may be related to God, or sin, or grace, or transcendence. The secular world, as we call it, lies within the sovereignty of God the Creator, and while Christians bring the challenge of God to it, God may in mysterious ways be there within it, bringing a challenge to them.

Yet no preaching or apologetic or exposition can avail without the community of men and women who live by the biblical faith, and exemplify its validity. The faith of both the Old Testament and the New is the faith of the people of God, and they are that faith's continuing witness. In spite of the countless failings of Christian institutions, there are Christians who show in their lives an openness of fellowship with one another, an openness of service to humanity, and an openness of humility and dependence towards God within and beyond. Such lives show a power to face suffering in the spirit of Christ, and to blend practical service within the world with an otherworldliness which suggests a heavenly destiny.

THE CLIMAX OF THE STORY   November 18

Christians say the Bible contains "the word of God", or "the revelation of God". But consider *how* this is so. Bibles were not rained down in a shower from heaven, some with Apocryphas and some without. No, the books of the Bible were written at many different dates and stages, but within the particular history of a particular people, the Jews, telling of the conviction that in the middle of this history and people God was uniquely making himself known.

In the Bible the rough and the smooth are inseparable. It is through a human people with its failings and perversities, through a human literature with its partial insights and responses, that we believe the divine word to have been spoken. The deliverance of the Jews from Egypt is believed throughout the story to be a divine act bringing them to freedom and privilege. The law and the covenant given by Moses link together privilege and responsibility. Then comes the series of prophets proclaiming in a crescendo of majestic messages that God is righteous, loving, holy, accessible to the humble soul, the ruler of all history, using Israel as a messenger to make him known to the other nations.

True, God has made himself partly known in many religions and cultures: but what is here unique is God showing himself as sovereign Creator who (in the poetic language which alone suffices) humbles himself to lift the simple from the dust. The theme is the sovereignty of God, shown in a particular history, and to be realised in a climax which will affect all history.

Jesus is the climax of *this* story. He is from the Jews. See how important that is for the understanding of him. If anything is historically certain about Jesus, this is: that he identified himself with the revelation of God to the Jews; their Bible was his Bible, their God was his God. But he endorsed this revelation not as complete in itself, but as a first volume in relation to which *he was himself the second volume.* (ICF)

TWO EYES OF FAITH   November 19

At a time when the Graeco-Roman culture was sick and disillusioned, the biblical faith, now summed up in the religion of the New Covenant, penetrated into it and revived it, blending the essence of Israel's faith with the forms of classical thought. Hence arose the new phenomenon, Christian humanism, which became the prevailing culture of Europe. By Christian humanism I mean a love of all things human, in art and science and literature, together with a recognition that beyond man there is a Creator and a Judge before whom he stands responsible, and that beyond this temporal existence there is an eternal life.

But let me emphasise specially that Christian humanism enables men and women to have a truly comprehensive idea of "nature". Nature includes all the phenomena which God has made: planets, plants, animals, birds, and man both in his affinity to the world with which he is bound up, and in his affinity to his creator, with the capacities for saintliness which this involves. The study of nature includes all this.

Recall one of those ancient churches where the carving on the capitals and gargoyles includes foliage, animal life, and scenes of ordinary human life (both dignified and grotesque), while the paintings on the walls include the stories of the Saviour and the saints, and over the chancel arch there is the great Doom, for beyond man there is a death and judgment.

Christian humanism was summed up by Thomas à Kempis when he said that the man of faith has two eyes, and discerns with his left eye the things of earth, and with his right eye the things of heaven. (DEA)

THE VENERABLE BEDE   November 20

There is something very non-ecclesiastical in the mode of Bede's sanctity and influence. No saint had less fuss made about him. His parentage is unknown, and so is his birthplace. No miracles are ascribed to him in his lifetime, and though the word *sanctus* was sometimes applied to him in subsequent centuries, little in the way of official *cultus* came to surround him. Indeed, he has been allowed, more than most saints, to be himself, and to be known and remembered in straightforward terms of humanity and history.

Benedict Biscop founded the monastery at Wearmouth in 674, and the sister house of Jarrow seven years later. To his care the boy Bede was entrusted by his parents at the age of seven, and thereafter Bede's whole life was spent in the houses of Wearmouth and Jarrow, with only two recorded journeys to other places. It was seemingly a very sheltered life, but, with the splendid libraries collected by Benedict Biscop, Bede missed few of the gales of thought and action which were blowing in England, and indeed in Europe. For its time, Bede's *Ecclesiastical History of the English People* was a scientific achievement. He wove together with delicate skill many different strands of tradition, he sifted with a not wholly uncritical eye the mass of wonder stories, and he conveyed to posterity much knowledge which would otherwise have perished.

Bede has less to say about the virtues of the monastic life than about the tasks of Christians as Christians. I recall a passage where, in discussing the office of a shepherd, he points out that not only bishops and priests are shepherds, but also every Christian who has a household to care for—however small—is a shepherd too.

WHOM DO YOU SAY I AM? November 21

Modernism or liberalism, in its proper meaning, is not a new-fangled eccentricity, but something inherent in Christianity, and the apostolic age knew it as the ceaseless effort to think out and to express the meaning of *Jesus is Lord* in different contexts of thought and culture as the Gospel moved across the world. Our Lord encouraged questioning and inquiry: "What think you?" "Whom do you say that I am?" "Why even of yourselves do you not judge what is right?" "How do you read?"

And later, all through the ardent missionary labours of the apostles, the asking of questions about the meaning of Jesus in relation to God and the world, and the meaning of God and the world in relation to Jesus, continued. The sheer mental vigour of the early Church was astonishing. Yet the process which was, in one aspect, search and discovery, was at the same time God-given. That was the other facet. "Flesh and blood did not reveal this to you, but my Father in heaven". "No one can come to me unless the Father draw him." All was God-given. And so the apostle says, "No man can say 'Jesus is Lord' except through the Holy Spirit".

The mind's understanding, the will's free choice, the heart's conviction, the mouth's confession, were possible only through an enabling divine power within a man. And here we have one of Christianity's paradoxes; all is of man's freedom, and yet all is of God's gift and rule. We must use our minds and reach conclusions; it is the Spirit who guides us. But in practice it helps us if we remember that the Holy Spirit is the Spirit of Jesus.

GOD CAN FACE RISKS   November 22

There is a kind of defensive Catholicism which supposes that no risks must be taken in the process of Christian unity, as if Catholic truth needed "protecting", whereas the gifts of God are powerful enough to vindicate themselves in the growing together of different traditions. The truth of God is greater than our efforts to conserve it.

So, too, there is a spirit of fearfulness which thinks that no good can ever come of movements which are outside the camp of Christendom, forgetting that God could use a Cyrus, an Assyria, or an altar-to-an-unknown-deity in his great purpose in history.

Whenever the exponents of the Christian faith treat it as something we have to "defend", like a beleaguered fortress, or a fragile structure, they are making God smaller than he is. (CPT)

VISIBLE UNITY   November 23

St. Paul, dealing with Corinth, was horrified that in the one *ecclesia* of God in Corinth there was a division between the adherents of Paul, the adherents of Peter, the adherents of Apollos. I think he would have been still more horrified if Christianity in

Corinth had come to be organised in a shape in which there was an *ecclesia* bearing the name of Paul, an *ecclesia* bearing the name of Peter, and so on. I hope that we are convinced that there is something which is really contrary to St. John 17—contrary both to that prayer that we may all be one, and the essential concept of the one *ecclesia* as understood in New Testament times.

It is contrary to visible unity if those things Christ has given to us for the very purpose of our one-ness should be labelled in separate denominational compartments. There is one baptism and I believe that Christians everywhere now do nothing contrary to the fact that there is one baptism. But there is also one eucharist, and there is something very wrong if there is the Presbyterian eucharist, the Anglican eucharist, and the Roman Catholic eucharist, fenced off from the others by labels into compartments.

Equally, is it meant that there should be *the* Christian ministry, *the* Christian bishop, *the* Christian priest? It is contrary to visible unity if these too are organised into denominational lables in such a way that they are prevented by those labels from having the true flow of spiritual life with one another. Perhaps it is not a question of building a structure so much as liberating ourselves and all Christians from structures which, alas, through the course of history have come to be divisive in character.

"DEAR CATHOLICS OF THE ROMAN OBEDIENCE"

November 24

The thought in my mind as I speak to you now, dear Christian people, dear Catholics of the Roman obedience, is not of our welcome to one another, but of Christ's welcome to us which the apostle emphasises as the secret of it all. When we say that unity must be in truth and holiness, we are saying that the secret of coming nearer to one another is that we should all of us become nearer to Christ. He welcomes us to an amazing nearness to himself; that is the secret if only we will receive his welcome.

Think how Christ welcomed you in your baptism and your confirmation. Think how he welcomes you in the Blessed Sacrament
with the scarcely believable intimacy of his real presence. Think
how he welcomes you in absolution when he washes your sins from
you just as he washed the feet of the apostles in the upper room.
Think how he welcomes you as you find him and are near to him in
the holy scriptures. It is an intimacy so aweful, so humbling. And
for all our sins and failings he welcomes us already into fellowship
with Blessed Mary and the saints in heaven as we join our prayers
and our praises with theirs in the Communion of Saints.

But what does this welcome demand of us? What is the practical
test of its validity? We know the answer. It is that we should actually
become Christlike: in humility, in generosity, in courage, in self-
forgetfulness. And that is why Christ's welcome to us always includes the privilege of suffering with him, if he wills it; of having
a little share in his Passion, of knowing that Calvary is a reality,
not only a name. But when we accept his welcome to all that, we
find the deep joy that marks the life of a Christian. We hear Jesus
saying to us, "These things have I said to you, that my joy may be
in you, and that your joy may be full".

In the Roman Catholic Cathedral at Westminster, 1968

WELFARE AND WITNESS   November 25

Let the Church, let every Christian, throw aside worldliness, pride
of status, pride of institution, and serve humanity: Christlike
Christians and a Christlike Church.

But we do need to look more deeply into what this means.
Already the revival of the idea of the servant Church is bringing
some misconceptions, not unlike those which appeared in connection with the ministry of Jesus.

Serving the world can all too easily be taken to mean giving the
world the things which it thinks it needs without challenging its
assumptions about what those needs are. In this way the Church

can try to commend itself as a kind of welfare society, advertising itself to the world on the world's own terms, instead of witnessing to the world's need for a radical conversion of its ideas, and for a knowledge of God's will which matters more than physical comfort.

Jesus never served the world more drastically than when he died on the Cross for its sake. (FFF)

SERVANTS AND SLAVES   November 26

In the New Testament writings there are two distinct Greek words which are commonly translated as "servant". The one is *diakonos* or deacon, and the corresponding verb. It is the word used in the teaching of Jesus at the Last Supper. It is a *functional* word. It means one who does certain acts towards others, in particular one who waits at table. Jesus does not sit to be waited upon; he waits upon his followers. The implication of this for us Christians is plain and overwhelming: we are called to the urgent practical service of the needs of the community.

The other word is *doulos*. It is properly translated as "slave". It expresses not function but *relationship*: belonging to someone, being owned by someone, and—in the context that we are discussing it—the someone is God or Christ.

It is strange that the *New English Bible*—perhaps through a lapse into a kind of donnish gentility—shrinks from the issue and translates the word as "servant". Slave is the meaning; no rights, no claims, but total possession by another. So St. Paul is Christ's slave, yielding himself to a Christ-possessed existence, and we are God's slaves as utterly belonging to him.

Of course the image does not exhaust the whole truth; we are God's sons and Christ's friends, and each image of itself is insufficient. But the image of *doulos* as slave speaks of that God-possession which belongs to our true relationship. "I come from God, I belong to God, I go to God."

So the Church serves humanity by being itself God-centred,

229

God-possessed, and witnesses that it is only through being possessed by God that mankind can find its true freedom. (FFF)

WITH THOSE WHO ARE OPPRESSED   November 27

It is rightly pointed out by biblical scholars that the liberation of mankind which Christ brings through the gospel is something deeper and wider than contemporary theologies of liberation sometimes suggest; for its essence is not the substitution of one social order for another, but the bringing of man himself into union with God in eternal life.

Nevertheless, Christianity is inevitably rejected if its exponents appear to stand on the side of privilege and injustice; and for the Church to be one with those who are oppressed is a part of its mission to be with the people where they are, with them and among them.

Only thus is the Church of Christ able credibly to witness that here we have no continuing city. (CP)

CULTURE AND CANDOUR   November 28

Now the essence of Christian fellowship—that is, the life of the *ecclesia*, or people of God—does not of necessity involve Gothic buildings, choirs and organs, pews and hassocks, and all the apparatus of ecclesiastical culture. It involves people, people united to Christ and to one another by the rites which he gave, and in the earliest years people met not in specialised buildings, but in one another's houses.

What are the essentials of a Church? To perpetuate the knowledge of Jesus by listening to his life and teaching and the apostolic witness to him; to recall Jesus in his ever-present sacrifice in the breaking of the bread; to praise the Father through him in the power of the Spirit; to practise fellowship; to serve the world; to draw people to Christ; and to help them on their way to heaven.

There are those who do this in the framework of the institutional culture which has lasted through the centuries with its appeal to eye and ear and memory and imagination. There are those who do this in houses and colleges and streets and factories. But let one thing be clear. It is a mistake to call the latter "non-Church" Christianity, for the meaning of Church is essentially the *ecclesia*, the people themselves. The phrase "experimental Christianity" is more accurate and helpful.

I have a feeling that one of the future tasks of Christian understanding and reconciling is going to be not between Catholic and Protestant Christianity so much as between "traditional" and "experimental" ways.

All of us who try to follow Christ must learn from one another with the humility which can listen, as well as the candour which can speak. (FFF)

RELIGIONLESS SELF-ABANDON?   November 29

There is among you, I well know, the passionate conviction that, in the words of St. James, "pure religion and undefiled is this: to visit the fatherless and widows in their affliction"—and not only the fatherless and widows, but the homeless, the hungry, the sick in mind and body, the victims of persecution and injustice.

With this conviction there often goes the suspicion that the whole business of prayer, pious practices, church services, contemplation, is a kind of hobby of remote religious culture. And the feeling comes that it may be right, in the name of Christianity itself, to put this hobby aside and to give oneself to the service of the world in a kind of religionless self-abandon, trusting that this will be nearer to Christ than any entrenched pious security. What do we say to this contrast?

I believe there has indeed been in our Christian civilisation a species of religious security which keeps the tragedies of the world at a distance, and utterly distorts the image of God who is the Father of Jesus and the Creator of the world. The revulsion from

231

this is laudable, and the revolt is understandable. Yet we Christians serve our fellows ill unless in the middle of our involvement with them we are witnessing to their need and our own need of that direct (call it "vertical" if you will) knowledge of God which demands quietness, contemplation, prayer, and sacrament.

Do not be afraid of the frankly otherworldly strain in Christianity. Do not be afraid of looking towards heaven, for heaven is the meaning of our existence as created in God's likeness for fellowship with him. And the quest of heaven is very far from being a pious escapism, inasmuch as the essence of heaven is selfless love, the same love which drives you to go without your dinner to help a family which has no food at all. (FFF)

THE ERADICATION OF SELFISHNESS   November 30

We still get the allegation that the doctrine of reward in heaven is selfish, although, as heaven is the perfection of persons in selfless love with one another and with God, it is hard to see how any selfish motive or ambition can bring us one step nearer to heaven.

Heaven is in essence the eradication of selfishness in the presence of God. Whenever Christians have thought otherwise, it has been a distortion of the teachings of the Beatitudes. (CP)

DECEMBER

THE INCARNATION December 1

It is an Anglican characteristic to make the Incarnation central in theology.

Now, making the Incarnation central has its dangers. There is always the danger of not giving enough emphasis to the doctrine of the Cross and redemption from sin, it has, I believe, been the essential role of the Evangelical element in Anglicanism to keep alive the emphasis upon the Cross—the reality of sin, forgiveness, atonement. In fact our theologians who have emphasised the Incarnation have themselves been men who have known very deeply what the Cross means, and of course wherever the Eucharist is central the Cross cannot fail to be central too. Nevertheless, the main trend of Anglican theology has been incarnational.

What has this meant in practice? Two things. One is that while Anglican theology has of course upheld the uniqueness of the Incarnation, it has also been ready to see the place of Christ in the cosmic process: Christ as both the climax of the operation of the divine Logos all through nature and history, and Christ as the heavenly Saviour breaking into the world. And in a new kind of way the emphasis on the cosmic Christ in Teilhard de Chardin is in line with a good deal of previous Anglican theology, though our theology has never risen to the deeply mystical way in which he grasps and expresses the truth.

The other thing the emphasis on the Incarnation has meant is this: that Anglican theology has again and again been ready—while upholding the uniqueness of Christ and the holy scriptures—to see the working of the divine Logos in the world around. For instance, when in the last century the belief in divine revelation found itself confronted by new developments in the secular sphere, like historical criticism, evolutionary biology, and so on, it did not say these things were of the devil. No, it was ready to say that these things are themselves part of the working of the divine Logos in the human mind, reason, and conscience, and it is possible for us to be learning from the contemporary world even where the world seems unpromising, because the divine Logos who is working in the world around us is the same Logos who is incarnate in Christ.

THE WORD AND THE PREACHER   December 2

The Word whom we preach is the Word who created the world, who sustains its order and beauty, who is ever at work in the ups and downs of history, whose coming in Jesus is the key to the whole.

To the preacher the realisation of this is at once shattering and consoling: shattering because the preacher's theme is so vast, its scope is reminiscent of the title of a medieval treatise, *De Omnibus Rebus et Quibusdam Aliis* (Concerning All Things and Certain Other Things as Well): consoling because behind the preacher is the almighty action of God in all things, and he is called not to be wise or powerful himself, but to bid his hearers listen to what God is saying in his ceaseless action in the world.

The Word is not imprisoned in a sermon; for it is present in its sovereign power before the preacher's mouth is opened, and after the preacher's lips are closed. (DEA)

234

There is one particular image which I ask you to look at closely. It is the image used by St. John which, more than any other, sums the matter up.

St. John writes, "The Word became flesh and dwelt among us, and we beheld his glory". *Word*: it is a biblical term, denoting one who is living, creative, imperishable, divine. *Flesh*: it is a biblical term denoting what is creaturely, frail, mortal, human. Here then is the paradox. The divine Creator has humbled himself to take on himself the entire experience of existence as man, in all the conditions of humanity.

Is it credible? It is only just credible. It is credible because there already exists the affinity between God and man, through man being made in God's likeness. This affinity anticipates the closest final fellowship conceivable between God and man.

Again, it is credible because of the infinity of God's love, with love's power of entering into the experience of another beyond all the analogies of love's power which we know. (ICF)

The righteousness of the kingdom is not a code of ethics: it is the response of men to God's presence, sovereignty, and goodness. Responding to God's providence, men will be trustful and not anxious. Responding to his generosity, they will be loving and forgiving to one another. Responding to his sovereignty they will renounce power, importance, and claims for themselves. The rich man can no more enter the kingdom than a camel can crawl through the tiny eye of a needle. Why? Because he is too big; he has power, importance in himself and his possessions. Little children are not too big: the kingdom is for them. He who exalts himself will be abased. It is God who reigns.

What is the role of Jesus himself in the coming of the kingdom? He speaks again and again not of a set of general principles, but of something which is happening, near and vivid. Decision is urgent. There can be no dallying. Here is the harvest. Reap it. Here is a priceless pearl. Buy it at once. A door is open. Hurry through it.

This urgency is because the "time" has arrived, the fulfilment, the end of an era: the old order is being wound up, a new order is breaking in. "Blessed are the eyes which see what you see. For I tell you many prophets and kings desired to see what you see, and did not see it, and to hear what you hear, and did not hear it."

The words *Jesus is Lord* formed the primitive creed of Christianity, and the core of the Christian faith.

Jesus: the word told of an historical person about whose life, words, and actions, much was known, and known not only in terms of the vehicle of a message, but in terms of a human figure whose example was to be imitated by Christian people. A version of Christianity which made the *Man* Jesus unknown or irrelevant must differ vastly from the primitive Christianity wherein the name of Jesus meant so much.

Is: the word told of one who belongs not only to the past, but to the contemporary because he had been raised from the dead: Jesus, "whom not having seen you love".

Lord: the word told of more than the Resurrection; it told of the sovereignty. Without becoming polytheists or idolaters the first Christians were led to be worshippers of Jesus, giving to him the kind of homage due from creatures to a creator.

Now we call this Christology, but no less significantly it was theology, for if there was a revolution in the attitude to Jesus who had been done to death by crucifixion, there was not less a revolution in the understanding of God and God's ways in the world.

Christology moved by a sure and inevitable process from *Christos* (Jesus as God's agent in history) to *Kurios* (Jesus as sovereign over the world) to *Logos* (Jesus as the total utterance of God and of the world's meaning). No less sure and inevitable was the movement of theology. A Jew who had believed in the reign of God in history can now, as a Christian, see the reign of God coming by means of a sacrificial death. A Greek who had believed in the unity and meaningfulness of the world in terms of an indwelling *logos* can now, as a Christian, see that unity and meaningfulness made known in Jesus. For both it was of supreme significance not only that Jesus was divine, but that God was Christlike.

INTERPRETATION NOW   December 7

Our contemporary task is the interpretation of *Jesus is Lord* in all the light and all the darkness which the modern world brings. We must be open to the lessons to be learnt from the contemporary world, and open also to the height and depth of the revelation of mercy and judgment in the Gospel.

We have radical questions to face. It is not only how we understand the story of Jesus in relation to God and man, and how we find Jesus to be meaningful. Rather are men and women asking how man is meaningful at all, and whether the idea of meaningfulness has any validity in the world in which we live.

As Christians we reply not primarily with certain types of thought or language, but with the fact of Jesus, and especially Jesus dying an ignominious death, and Jesus convincing man of his life after death. And clinging to this fact we say, "Here is meaningfulness, here is man in his true meaning, here is what we mean by God, here is sovereignty in a seemingly chaotic world."

I suggest to you that as the Cross and the Resurrection were the spearhead of the gospel's relevance and potency in the first century, so they can be also for our contemporary world.

Ours is a world full of suffering and frustration: of what significance to it is Jesus, who lived and died nearly two thousand years ago? The answer is chiefly in this, that in the death and resurrection he shows not only the way for man, but also the very image of God himself.

Is there within or beyond our suffering and frustrated universe any purpose, way, meaning, sovereignty? We answer, yes, there is purpose, way, meaning, sovereignty; and the death and resurrection of Jesus portray it as living through dying, as losing self to find self, as the power of sacrificial love. To commit oneself to this way is to be near the secret of God's own sovereignty, near to the power which already wins victories over evil, and will ultimately prevail.

That is the point at which Jesus can be shown to be near to our own world; and when he is found to be near at this point, then his life and teaching are found to have their compelling fascination. Through the life and teaching there runs the principle, "He who exalts himself shall be abased, and he who humbles himself shall be exalted". Through the life and teaching there is the strange blending of authority and humility. (CPT)

THE ESSENCE OF ALL GOOD   December 9

We exist in order that we may become like God, have intercourse with God, "give glory" to God. This is sometimes called "worship" —but see how deep and wide it goes. It means loving God above all else for the perfection that is his, but, because he *is* perfect love, our love for him is reflected in our love and our practical service of our fellows in community.

But because it is all his gift, and we are utterly dependent upon him, our love of our fellows brings us back again to give glory to God—the source of all good, the essence of all good.

Is it surprising that a matter that cuts so deep and wide should call for its own vocabulary? The word "glorify" is a great Christian word. It includes both the becoming like God so as to reflect him, and the reverent dependence upon him which befits a creature. It is from this that we all find ourselves shrinking, Christians and non-Christians alike. We like to be proud: it is the humble dependence which hurts our pride. (ICF)

DOUBLE EXISTENCE   December 10

One of the great images for the Church is the *Body of Christ*. You see how literal this is. Jesus risen from the dead and alive today has a body through which he lives and works and makes himself known, and this body is the Christian people. "You are the body of Christ", says the apostle.

The Church's own members have a double existence; they also belong to a race which is created and creaturely, illuminated by conscience, and subject to natural law.

Their possession of the new glorious status does not lead them to think themselves "above" the old status of a child of Adam. Far from it. Being under grace enables them the more to know themselves as creatures alongside their fellow creatures guided by law.

Being now the heirs of a supernatural sanctity, they are the more able to stoop to ally themselves to whatsoever is good, true, lovely, of good report—if there be any virtue, if there be any praise—among their fellows. That is how Christians are the salt of the earth: they season civilisation to be its best in terms of justice, order, and decency. (DEA)

A REDEEMED WORLD   December 11

The world is a redeemed world—it is not only the Church which is redeemed. What does this really mean? Is it just a rhetorical paradox of the theologian?

We need to be concrete and empirical. Society since Christ—both when unconverted and when converted—is affected by the presence within the universe of the risen Christ and his Church in paradise and on earth. It is subject to inroads of Christian influence. These may not be enough to make Christian assumptions the dominant assumptions, but they are enough to keep alive the perceptions of conscience and natural law.

The pond of civilisation is dirty and befouled, but it is not stagnant: movements of a cleaner water from time to time stir it. For instance, the totalitarian portion of the world in our time is not merely savage and amoral, it is also embarrassingly interfered with by at least some few perceptions of conscience, of the light that lighteneth, because the whole world is a world not only created but also redeemed by God. There is always the likelihood that *someone* will listen, even in the most unpromising contexts. (DEA)

FREEDOM IN THE NAME OF CHRIST   December 12

As Christians we must be the sworn foes of persecution, of arbitrary imprisonment, of racial discrimination, of crippling poverty and hunger. We shall throw ourselves into these causes of freedom in the name of Christ, and our Christian discipleship will be tested by our practical concern for our fellows. But we shall be aware that while these issues are easily stated in terms of freedom *from*, awkward questions arise when we go on to ask what is the freedom *for*.

History shows that communities can be well fed, prosperous, and highly cultured, liberal and democratic as well, enjoying a host of the freedoms we care about, and yet be a prey to selfishness, self-indulgence, indecent luxury, domestic unhappiness, and—so far from being mentally free—can be at the mercy of contemporary blasts of sentiment and folly. We know what we want to free men from. Do we know what we want to free men for?

Our striving as Christians for the freedoms which most palpably stir our feelings is always in the context of the more radical and revolutionary issue of the freeing man from self—a freedom whose goal is heaven, and whose reflection is in a thousand actions here and now.

Here each one of us starts with himself and his own need for freedom from self and into the glory of God. You can shout and protest on behalf of freedom on this issue and that, and yet be evading the Divine Protest which is addressed to each of us. (FFF)

POST-MORTEM JUDGMENT   December 13

The crucifixion of Jesus brings *judgment*. When we look at the reactions of the followers of Jesus in the years following the event, we find something quite remarkable. Usually when a tragedy has happened there is subsequently a kind of *post-mortem* reflection upon it. "Could it have been avoided?" "Surely it could have been avoided if only so-and-so had acted differently." "I can never forgive X or Y for what he did."

The tragedy of the death of Jesus gave immense scope for that sort of post-mortem talk on the part of those who loved him. Certain people were obviously to blame: the priests who plotted; Judas who betrayed; Pilate who weakly acquiesced. Yet very early the Christian view was not to point a finger of blame at the enemy who had done this deed in contrast with themselves who would never have done such a thing. No: they said in effect, "We are *all* guilty. Judgment is upon *all* of us". (ICF)

GETTING TO GRIPS   December 14

The particular vocation of a monk or nun to poverty, chastity, obedience is but one form of the vocation every single Christian has at his baptism: to be poor in spirit, to be pure in heart, to obey the Lord Jesus and his Church.

It is terribly hard to put into words just what this holiness means. It is a matter of you and your relation to our Lord: how you are towards him in the depths of your being. And the secret is your readiness to face up to the truth about yourself over against our Lord who loves you and died for you. In a word, *penitence*. If you get to grips with the business of penitence you are on the way the saints have trod; if you shirk penitence you may be stuck for ever.

With Christmas approaching very near, I charge every one of you, layman or deacon or priest, as indeed I have to charge myself, to make before this Christmas the most thorough penitence we have ever made. An old writer, the son of Sirach, said, "There is a shame that leadeth to sin: and there is a shame which is for grace and glory". Make your own the shame which is for grace and glory.

We see the shame when one who was a sinner bathed the feet of Jesus with her tears and wiped them with her hair. We see the glory when Mary, and countless others down the ages, chose the good part not to be taken from them in this world or the next. Through this shame and to this glory may God in his mercy lead us all. (DEA)

THE LAST JUDGMENT   December 15

What about the Last Judgment? Christ, at the end of his public teaching, gave two parables about judgment. One is called the parable of the talents. It describes the judgment in store for those who possess Christian privileges. They will be judged by the use they have made of the gifts given to them. A stern judgment awaits those who have not used the gifts at all. Christians, that is the judgment for us.

The other is called the parable of the sheep and goats. It describes the judgment upon the Gentiles—the outsiders, the people who have not been within the Christian covenant. They are judged by their practice of the natural virtues of kindness—to the naked, to the sick, to strangers, to prisoners—and if they have been good to the naked, the sick, the strangers, the prisoners, they have all unknowing been near to God, and have been doing kindness to Christ himself. (ICF)

HEAVEN AND HELL   December 16

Heaven and hell are called the last things. But they are anticipated daily in the here and now. Every act of faith and charity, every movement of heart and mind towards God, is an anticipation of heaven. The Christian Eucharist is a little sharing in heaven's worship, and the Holy Spirit working in us is the first fruits of the heavenly inheritance, the power already of the age to come.

So too is hell anticipated whenever men isolate themselves in pride and selfishness, and make barriers between one another, and between them and their Creator. Our life as Christians is one of conflict and ambiguity: we live under grace, and yet sin dies very hard within us.

Thus heaven and hell already do battle, and the conflict between them may be raging within our prayers as well as in our actions. (CEA)

WHAT OF HELL?   December 17

In either case—the believer's or unbeliever's—what of hell? There is the love of God for all of us. There is our freedom. This freedom is the mark of our dignity, the mark of a universe based on love and not on pure mechanism; it is the condition of morality. I am free. The possibility is there that, in the face of all that the love of God does to win me through the years, I may yet persist to the last in choosing self-love, and in calling white black, and in creating for myself the final isolation.

What is hell? It is the self-chosen loneliness of the man or woman who prefers this to the love of God. The descriptions of it given in the Gospels may be partly coloured by conventional Jewish imagery, and we remember that Christ often used the language of

243

poetry: the burning fire, the gnawing worm. We don't know how many—if any—are there; or whether it involves the continuance or the extinction of consciousness. But we cannot explain away Christ's warnings, and am I not to apply these warnings to myself? I need to pray. What shall I pray for? That God will keep me safe.

> King of Majesty tremendous,
> Who dost free salvation send us,
> Fount of pity, thou befriend us.
> Think, kind Jesus, my salvation
> Caused thy wondrous Incarnation,
> Leave me not to reprobation.

"God keep me safe." But "safe" does not mean secure in a comfortable box of piety: it means sharing in the outgoing love of God, now, and at the last. (ICF)

IN DARKNESS   December 18

The credibility of hell rests upon the concept of human freedom. Our freedom is the condition of our human dignity, of our being creatures who are not automata, but can will to love or not to love. It is the condition of our place in a world based on love and not upon mechanism, of our adherence to an ethical theism.

I am free. Rob me of my power to separate myself from the love of God and to shut myself in darkness, and you rob me of the freedom whereby I know myself as the child and creature of the holy Father. This exclusion is hell, the self-exclusion of those who prefer to be isolated in self-love because they want it so to be. Theoretically it is hard to see how the loss can be eternal, for—as F. D. Maurice insisted—eternity is the quality of God and of the life shared with him. Theoretically it could be everlasting. But is it? We have to ask what has been revealed by Christ.

Christ describes the loss and punishment of those excluded from him at the judgment, and the adjective in the Gospels is αἰώνιος which some would translate "everlasting", and other "of the aeon to come". We are reckoning with imagery, and imagery is poetical. We need not be compelled to take literally the fire and the gnawing worm, nor perhaps the language of duration. We know that there was a tendency in the early Church to elaborate the imagery of the apocalyptic in the tradition of the word of Jesus, as a comparison of some parallel passages in St. Mark and St. Matthew shows.

Yet, when full allowance has been made for sayings which are poetic rather than literal, and for the possibility of elaborations in the Gospel tradition, it is impossible to eliminate sayings of Jesus which give terrible warnings as to the possibility of loss and exclusion. Warnings against loss of salvation are there, incisive and inexorable. What the state of loss may be like, or how many may be lost, we do not know. It is one of those matters where our Lord seems to give us not definitions, nor answers to our curiosity, but warning and challenge.

"Are there few that be saved?" he is asked, and our Lord answers, "Strive to enter by the strait gate". We put the warning to ourselves. (CEA)

GLORIOUS FREEDOM   December 19

When the apostle Paul speaks of the "glorious freedom of the children of God" he is thinking of the final goal of heaven in which freedom is perfectly realised.

In all our thinking and acting about freedom, we bear in mind the final reference. The different aspects of freedom which we cherish and realise in this life are fragmentary anticipations of the freedom which is heaven itself. Yet the freedom derived from Jesus begins now. It is here, real and creative.

We remember indeed that Christ hated injustice and oppression, and we as Christians will be uncompromisingly against injustice among ourselves and the wider world. So now let the Christmas message of simplicity come home to us. Let us reverse the processes of looking for higher and higher standards, and resolve that enough is enough, and luxuries are unnecessary: that many of us can be as happy—or happier—with less.

Christ became poor, Christ chose the way of simplicity, and if we follow him he promises us riches of his own, riches of a happiness and a brotherhood shared with one another and with him. (CP)

SIMPLICITY   December 20

We ought not to exaggerate or to sentimentalise the poverty of Christ. There is no suggestion in any of the Gospels that Christ was ever destitute or in abject penury. Joseph had a trade, and Jesus grew up in the security of a happy home. We know that he shared in social pleasure, and enjoyed at times being both a guest and a host.

But the characteristic which gave him the title "poor" was *simplicity*. Again and again he struck the note of simplicity. He did without many things that people crave for. None did he criticise more severely than those who hankered after more and more possessions, and those who were preoccupied with money. The worth of a man's life, he insisted, does not consist in the things that he has; his worth is not increased by piling up and piling up. People matter more than things, for people have an eternal destiny. And those who do not fuss about their standard of living can serve one another, and enjoy one another as people. (CP)

ST. THOMAS'S DAY   December 21

The evangelist tells us that Thomas was not with the others on the first Easter evening; he missed the first of the Easter appearances. He had not seen the Lord, and when he heard the story he was sceptical. Was it really true or was it fantasy? He brooded. He hesitated. His eyes must see, his hands must touch the wounds of Jesus.

A week later, on what we now call Low Sunday, the chance comes. Jesus is with them. And Thomas is with them too. Jesus offers the doubter all he has asked for, and more. Thomas, come and see, come and touch. And Thomas will not wait to accept what the Lord offers him; his heart, his mind, and his voice leap ahead, ahead of any declaration of faith that any of the disciples had made: My Lord and my God. And the answer of Jesus reaches beyond Thomas to all of us: Thomas saw and believed, and all of us are happy because without ever having seen, we believe all the same.

So to all of us the last Beatitude is spoken. Happy are you, you in any century, you in any place, you in any part of the world, you perhaps who are in cruel grief or sorrow, you perhaps who are bewildered and frustrated: happy are you, happy because, though you do not see Jesus, your Easter faith is sure. (CP)

CHRISTMAS DIVIDES   December 22

Christmas says that Christ was born in the simplicity of Bethlehem, and luxury and wealth and worldly power and success are irrelevant to man's true blessedness. In response, men and women may recapture the true simplicity of human life, or they may scorn it by pursuing all those false values which Bethlehem condemns. In this way Christmas divides.

It divides the followers of Christ from those who are not his followers at all. More poignantly it divides Christians from Christians: Christians whom Christ can recognise, and Christians whose ways are sadly far from their profession. Yes, Christmas pierces into the consciences of all of us, with our many conflicts of ideal and practice, of response and failure. And the child born at Bethlehem is indeed set for the rise and fall of many.

WHAT WE WANT MOST   December 23

What different needs there are when one thinks about different scenes in different countries and continents! There it is food; there it is freedom; here it is peace and unity; there it is this or that material comfort or advantage.

But again and again in human affairs there is this distinction: there is the thing a man thinks he wants most, and there are the things he really needs most—whether or not he consciously wants them.

I may, most of all, want this or that—and how lovely it would be if it were to arrive as a Christmas present in my stocking. But other people may know—and God my Creator certainly does know—that the thing I need most may be something I hardly realise I need: some virtue I badly lack, or the removal of some fault I like to ignore, or some opportunity or impulse to serve my fellows in some new and exciting way.

My wants: they are apt to be on the surface. My need: that is apt to be deeper—it may be very deep in the depths of my being.

PIERCING CHALLENGE   December 24

The Christmas event at Bethlehem is not a kind of idyllic scene of cosy comfort, as if to say, "Come to Bethlehem, turn in here, visit the stable of the nativity and have some peace just for a while". Rather does the Christmas scene confront the world with a sharp, piercing, and painful challenge.

Mary the Mother knew this. She had known this when she sang the *Magnificat*, telling of the putting down of the mighty from their seat and the exalting of the humble and meek. And she knew it when, some days after the child's birth, she brought him into the temple to present him to God, and the aged Simeon took the child into his arms and said, "This child is set for the fall and the rise of many, and for a sign that shall be spoken against".

First in Israel, and subsequently in every country where the news of Christ travelled, it would bring sharp division: some would rise and some would fall; some would respond in faith, and some would find themselves under judgment, and the hearts of men and women would be exposed so as to make it plain where they stood. The sword of division was to Mary herself a sword of grief and sorrow.

THE ANSWER OF CHRISTMAS   December 25

It is because we believe that God has an answer to man's predicament, the answer of the Word-made-flesh at Bethlehem, that we have hope, and, having hope, are rejoicing once again at Christmas.

Christians for whom this hope is a reality have been able to rejoice even when they have been in the world's darkest places. It was in prison in Rome, with the prospect of death awaiting him, that St. Paul wrote, "Rejoice, and again I say, rejoice . . . In nothing be anxious, the Lord is at hand".

The proof of our Christian hope is the existence of men and women who have lived by it, and have radiated its joy even in dark and heartbreaking circumstances. Each of us will have known such men and women, and it is in them that Christmas is seen to be alive.

The child born as on this day is set for the rising and falling of many, and when today the sword of Bethlehem pierces our own souls, may it find us on the side of those who know the costly secret of Christmas joy.

WHAT CHRISTMAS SAYS   December 26

Our Christmas is no less Christmas, and our joy is no less joyful, because we are keeping Christmas with a very dark and troubled world around us. We cannot banish from our minds the miseries in the poorer countries; the continuing griefs of political and racial strife; the many in the world who are without homes or without food; the many who are lonely, and without friends to cheer them.

Our rejoicing at Christmas is not an escape from life's grim realities into a fancy realm of religion and festivity. Rather is it a joy that, as we face and feel the world's tragedy, we know that God has an answer: an answer for mankind to receive. In a word, this is a time of hope.

Christmas says: Christ has taken humanity to himself, and so every man and woman and child in the world is lovable and infinitely precious. And, in response, men and women can treat one another—whatever their race or colour—in the light of Bethlehem; or they can, in rejecting the human dignity of their fellows, reject their own dignity too.

A MOVEMENT ONWARDS   December 27

What is the destiny of a Christian?

Christ and the apostles give us some clear intimations in their teaching. Christ said to the thief who was dying, crucified near to him in his own last dying hours, "Today, you shall be with me in paradise".

Paradise did not mean a place of final perfection. Literally meaning a park, it was a word used comprehensively of the place of all departed spirits who are not lost. "With me": the thief who died was to be with Jesus, and plainly this means a conscious existence with human fellowship and fellowship with God.

But it is not revealed to us that after death perfection is immediately attained. The fact of God's holiness, and the need for us to become holy like him, precludes the idea that the mere event of death enables a sort of moral jump from our present imperfection to a final perfection. Hence, we believe in growth, a purgation, a movement onwards, a being made perfect, after death. And if in this there is the pain of purgation, there is (can we doubt?) the joy of the growing fellowship with Christ. (ICF)

FOR EVER AND EVER   December 28

A lady once came to me in great distress because, whenever she went to church, she kept hearing the words which upset her: the words "for ever and ever".

The words gave her the creeps: "for ever and ever", "for ever and ever". A terrible thought indeed! But the Christian hope is not just that we shall have our existence prolonged for ever. Christianity shares indeed with the philosophy of Plato the belief in survival after death; but what is significant in Christianity is not a life of endless duration, but a life in fellowship with God through union with Christ.

It is the life dreamed of by the psalmist when he said, "God is the strength of my life, and my portion for ever". It is the life described by St. John, "This is the life eternal, to know thee the one true God, and Jesus Christ whom thou hast sent". It is the life which Christ mediates to those who, united to him, have him as their centre. "Because I live, ye shall live also."

To belong to Christ is to possess eternal life now already, and to hope for its completion after death. (ICF)

ALREADY, AND NOT YET   December 29

Already the Christians united with Christ are raised together with him. Already they are partakers of Christ, possessors of his life-giving Spirit, sharers in eternal life. St. Paul and St. John are at one in affirming this present realisation.

But there is a "not yet", and a consummation still to come. Though they are already "in Christ", the Christians are still living in this world, they belong to cities, states and nations. They are involved in suffering, and in sin which contradicts their Christian status. But in this ambiguous interim they await a future glory. It will be an unveiling in perfection of a union with Christ at present hidden and incomplete. It will be "the coming of Christ", "the resurrection", "the glory". It must be wrong to try to be literalistic about the imagery used to express the inexpressible, for "eye hath not seen, nor ear heard, neither have entered into the heart of man the things which God hath prepared for them that love him".

Thus, through the doctrine of resurrection in the New Testament, with its double strain of something already realised and something not yet, we approach the doctrine of heaven. Here let the word "glory" guide us in our approach. It is one of the marvellous words of the Bible, for it tells of heaven and the last things, and it also tells of man and the first things. So it is; God created man in his own image in order that he might come to perfect fellowship with his Creator. It is a fellowship of intimacy, love, and knowledge, intermingled with awe and dependence; of man reflecting the Creator's character, and humbly ascribing all to him, which the Bible describes by the words *glory* and *glorify*.

There is the secret of man's existence, and of his role in the created world, and the clue to man's destiny. Heaven is the final consummation of this, for heaven is man finding himself in the glory of his Maker. (CEA)

HARMONY AND VISION   December 30

Heaven! We know that analogies fail us, that prose can say little, that poetry and symbol are less misleading, that our conceptions of time and duration fail. But we know that the Creator made us to worship him and to reflect his likeness, and heaven will be the perfection of that.

The antitheses which so often disturb us will be resolved. Worship and service will be one. Activity and rest will find harmony. The triumph of achievement and the fascination of new discovery will be blended. There will be the vision of God in whom is the perfection of beauty, wisdom, love. This is how St. Augustine describes heaven: "We shall rest and we shall see, we shall see and we shall love, we shall love and we shall praise, in the end which is no end".

But because God is love and heaven is our perfection in love, there is no heaven for him who cherishes a kind of private ambition: "I want heaven". That is why the idea that the Christian heaven can be a sort of selfish compensation is utterly beside the mark. Further-more, because heaven is what it is, you cannot dream of your own perfection there apart from the perfection of others. (ICF)

WITH THE LORD OF THE DEAD AND THE
LIVING   December 31

Heaven is the goal of man, and heaven gives the true perspective for our present life. Our belief in the goal of heaven goes with our belief in the infinite and eternal worth of every man, woman, and child created in God's own image, and reminds us that we are called to nothing less than the Christ-like perfection of the saints.

In the Communion of Saints, which is the family of Jesus, the Lord of the dead and the living, we are one with the saints in every age, and in that oneness with them we hold fast to the truth which belongs to no one age because it is timeless. In the Communion of Saints we are freed from the dominance of the contemporary, as well as of the past. We shall know "the glorious liberty of the children of God".